# Chalk Dust

# PRAISE FOR CHALK DUST

"Eager young educators and preservice teachers will see themselves in Curby Alexander's *Chalk Dust*. By sharing his own story, he speaks into the hearts of everyone who played school with their stuffed animals and to those of us who found teaching in a profound "Aha!" moment later in life. His warm, conversational style feels like a really good chat with your favorite uncle. He is the vulnerable, helpful mentor we all needed at the beginning of our careers."

—AMBER ESPING, Associate Professor of Educational Psychology, Texas Christian University

"Part memoir, part love letter to teachers finding their way in an increasingly demanding profession, this book has something for everyone—the veteran reflecting on a career or the young person wondering about a career in teaching. It's a must-read that provides a valuable window into the journey of teaching."

—JO BETH JIMERSON, William L. and Betty F. Adams Chair of Education, Texas Christian University

# Chalk Dust

## REFLECTIONS FROM A TEACHER'S FIRST YEAR

### CURBY ALEXANDER

FORT WORTH, TEXAS

Copyright © 2024 by Richard Curby Alexander

Library of Congress Control Number: 2023943670

TCU Box 298300
Fort Worth, Texas 76129
817.257.7822

Design by Preston Thomas, Cadence Design Studio

# Contents

| | | |
|---|---|---|
| PREFACE | | vii |
| PROLOGUE | THE CHAOS GAME | 1 |
| CHAPTER 1 | THE BOX | 9 |
| CHAPTER 2 | ALONE | 17 |
| CHAPTER 3 | PLACE | 23 |
| CHAPTER 4 | IN LOCO PARENTIS | 29 |
| CHAPTER 5 | FUZZY | 34 |
| CHAPTER 6 | CRACKS | 50 |
| CHAPTER 7 | SPAGHETTI | 61 |
| CHAPTER 8 | THE COMPARISON TRAP | 70 |
| CHAPTER 9 | ARROWS | 76 |
| CHAPTER 10 | CONFERENCES WITH PARENTS | 81 |
| CHAPTER 11 | SONGS AND STORIES | 87 |
| CHAPTER 12 | PROXY | 96 |
| CHAPTER 13 | IMPOSTER | 101 |
| CHAPTER 14 | COMMUNION | 111 |
| CHAPTER 15 | BUSTED | 115 |
| CHAPTER 16 | REPAIRED | 120 |
| CHAPTER 17 | BOXES | 127 |
| CHAPTER 18 | OUT OF THE SHADOWS | 130 |
| EPILOGUE | DEAR CURBY | 132 |
| ACKNOWLEDGEMENTS | | 139 |
| ABOUT THE AUTHOR | | 142 |

# PREFACE

FOUR YEARS DIDN'T FEEL LIKE ENOUGH TIME. Within that span, I managed to earn a teaching degree, but there was no way to fit in everything I would need to know. Life after college had its share of disappointment, loneliness, and disillusionment, but it was also perhaps my time of greatest growth. This is the story of me traveling halfway across the country with nothing more than a diploma to begin my career as a teacher. From the moment I crossed the threshold into my empty classroom, through the process of learning to cope with feelings of isolation and incompetence, to the small victories of hope and laughter that kept me going, my story is an invitation into the heart and mind of a first-year teacher. These experiences were more than events; they became the connective tissue that gave my career form and meaning, and my memories are like chalk dust at the end of a long day of teaching, subtle reminders of purposeful hard work, the value of lifelong learning, and the power of human connection.

# PROLOGUE: The Chaos Game

"TEACHING IS MY CALLING."

"I want to inspire my students like my teachers inspired me."

"As a child, I used to teach lessons to my dolls and stuffed animals, explaining concepts on my whiteboard and grading their papers. That was when I knew I was destined to become a teacher."

"I don't teach for the income. I teach for the outcome."

"Teaching is not just requiring children to memorize random facts. It's about changing children's lives."

"I didn't choose teaching. Teaching chose me."

Each semester I assign a paper where my students, the majority of whom are preparing for a career in education, explain why they want to be a teacher. Many students were inspired to pursue this career because of impactful teachers they had in the past. Others were the children of teachers, and they have seen firsthand the difference they can make in the lives of students. Some students have a passion for a particular subject and want to pass on the torch of learning, and I've even had students choose teaching because it seems like a lot of fun. Unlike other professions, teachers often find themselves explaining, rationalizing, and justifying their decision for choosing this career. To my knowledge, realtors and bankers don't have to write a philosophy statement, but for some reason teachers must be able to articulate why they want to do this job. By extension, I find myself trying to do so each time I read these papers, reflecting on the series of mishaps and breakthroughs leading me into a career as an educator.

While at an education conference, I listened to a math educator talk about a gadget he developed that would simulate what he called the "chaos game." In his demonstration, he started with an equilateral triangle and plotted a point randomly inside its borders. He then measured halfway between the point and one of the three vertices, where he plotted another point. One after another, he plotted about a dozen points halfway between the previous dot and one of the vertices. He stopped the demonstration and asked everyone to predict what would happen if he did this one hundred, one thousand, or ten thousand more times. The existing points looked random to me, so I predicted more points would just look like a huge mess. Using his gadget, the presenter sped the process up to plot ten thousand points in a matter of seconds. The result was not only surprising, but it was also beautiful and amazing. He called this phenomenon the Sierpinski's Gasket, and the result was a fractal: an intricate design of perfectly symmetrical equilateral triangles, nested facsimiles of the original shape.

I don't remember the exact thoughts I had during the presentation, but when I walked away, I remember contemplating, *What is it about Sierpinski's Gasket that won't leave me alone?* At the heart of this concept were questions that had been nagging at me for years: How did my life end up like this? How did all the high and low points—all my good and bad decisions along the way—eventually become my life?

I stumbled into my career as an educator. As a student in elementary and high school, I would watch what the teacher was doing and think, *That would be pretty cool. I think I could be a teacher.* Then I would look around me at how the other students in my class were misbehaving, and think, *On second thought . . .* At times, I contributed to the misbehavior, and I wondered if I might be repaid the consequences of my own deeds. There was also the issue of ability. I was mainly a compliant student who did what I was told. My work was turned in on time, I usually didn't talk or cause problems for the teacher, and I got along with everyone in my class. But I never had a burning passion for any particular subject area, unless you counted music, and I had already ruled that out as a career choice.

During my first year of college, I got a job at a grant-funded preschool on my campus. I was hired to wash the dishes from breakfast and lunch. The job was pretty easy, and it gave me a chance to sneak handfuls of Life cereal between cycles on the industrial dishwasher. One day the preschool director came in to make a request. The staff was a little short-handed, and she wanted to know if I would be interested in reading to the children who didn't take a nap or who woke up early, so they wouldn't disrupt the other children. How hard could this be, right? So each day I would finish washing the lunch trays faster and faster, so I had more time to read to the children in a small room just off the main room of the preschool. As a theatre major, I did my best to make the books come alive by using funny voices and sound effects. It wasn't long before the director asked me if I wanted more hours at the center by coming in and supervising the children whose parents worked late. The next thing I knew, I was a professional babysitter.

This job just happened to coincide with an English class I was taking. I wasn't a standout student, but I was a decent writer. I wrote for the school newspaper and worked on the yearbook staff in high school. When registering for my first semester of college courses, I decided to challenge myself and take an advanced English composition class. This was the only subject in high school in which I took advanced placement (AP) courses, so I felt up for the challenge. The instructor challenged me all right, but more than that she helped me find my voice and a love for writing. I actually looked forward to writing assignments.

At the time all of this was happening, a part of me was growing discontent. Most of my friends had left my hometown to attend college in other parts of the country. Some went to big state universities, while others went to private schools in Illinois, Minnesota, Iowa, Colorado, Nebraska, and California. This wasn't a big deal the summer before everyone left, but when they came back for Thanksgiving and Christmas, I heard them talk about their adventures and was able to see for the first time what I was missing. I was attending the local community college in my hometown, which was not only less than five minutes from my parents' house, but it was also where they both worked. It was a good school, but it was like going to summer camp in your backyard. In the span of a couple of weeks, I went from thinking my situation was pretty good to being miserable, wanting nothing more than to go somewhere else . . . anywhere else.

My parents finally conceded to let me investigate some different schools that we thought were affordable, were far enough to satisfy my desire to be away from home, and had programs of study in which I was interested. After extensive research and number crunching, I chose Utah State University as my destination. And this was when all of the circumstances in my life seemed to start lining up. I never envisioned myself as a teacher, but I was convinced the intersection of my love for writing and interest in helping children was leading me to a career in writing textbooks. I should mention, my backup plan was going to law school and joining the FBI. Hmm . . . textbook writing or the FBI? My career aspirations were obviously in their formative stages and shifting with the infamous Wyoming wind.

As anyone who has taken education classes can attest, schools of education don't really train people to write textbooks. They train people to become teachers. My school just so happened to believe that extensive field experience was a major ingredient in this training, so rather than learning how to write textbooks, I spent a lot of my time in classrooms throughout the Cache Valley. Sometimes it was for a couple of hours, and all I did was observe. Other times it was for whole days, even weeks, at a time, and I would work with students in a variety of settings. I even got to plan a couple of lessons and deliver them to the whole class. And if the teacher happened to leave the room, I would try to be funny, disrupting whatever level of productivity she had been able to establish with the students. Just as the preschool job grew on me, the longer I worked there, these field experiences began to influence my self-perception. I started to see myself—dare I say—as a teacher.

One of my friends from high school had graduated from college a year before me. During my student teaching year, she was teaching music at an elementary school in Colorado. I visited her one weekend, and I was captivated with her life as a teacher as she showed me around the quaint ski town she now called home and shared stories about her first year as an educator. A year prior, I was still harboring my secret desire to apply for law school and try to get a job in the FBI (the textbook dream died slowly and quietly). Now, with graduation only a few months away, I was starting to think about where, and how, to apply for teaching jobs. I thought that if I could land in a cool ski town in Colorado, like my friend, this could be a pretty great gig.

As I started the nearly seven-hour drive back to Logan, I remembered an email from my mother telling me she was going to have a long layover at the Salt Lake City airport. She had been in Dallas leading a Christian ladies conference, and she gave me her flight information in case I was able to stop in and have coffee with her. Normally, I wouldn't have made the hour-and-a-half drive to Salt Lake City to have an hour-long coffee break, but I happened to be driving past the airport around the same time as her layover, so I stopped and waited for her flight to arrive.

I will never forget her first words as she got off the plane: "You will never believe what just happened." These words are not uncommon coming from my mom. Her life has been one of chance encounters and divinely arranged relationships. She proceeded to tell me that while at the Dallas Fort Worth airport with my uncle, her gate was suddenly changed to a different terminal. My uncle decided to go with her to the new gate so they could visit some more. While on the tram, the conversation shifted to me as my uncle probed my mom on what I was up to, and more importantly, what I planned on doing after graduation. She began to tell him that I was about to complete the requirements for my degree in elementary education, but no one, including me, knew what I was going to do after that.

Just then a man on the tram had looked up and walked across to where my mom and uncle were standing. He asked, "Did I just hear you say your son is an elementary education major?" He then introduced himself as the head recruiter for Grapevine-Colleyville Independent School District, and they were looking for men who were interested in teaching elementary school. He told her a little more about the school district and handed her an informational packet to give me. Just as he was handing her the packet, the tram stopped and he got off to catch his flight. All of the recruiter's claims about this school district were confirmed by my uncle, and he emphasized to my mother that if I had any interest in coming to Texas to teach, this was one of the best school districts to be in. I hadn't yet gone public with my intent to teach in a small Colorado ski town while working undercover as an FBI operative. I would hear what my mom had to say and talk about my real plans later.

This was when my mom handed me the folder she had received just two hours earlier. She told me this man would be at the job fair I was attending in a month or so, and he wanted me to look for him. I stuffed the folder in my backpack, and basically forgot about it for several weeks. As is the case for many college students, items that go in the backpack didn't always find their way out again. I'm thankful this folder eventually found its way back into my hands.

I was standing in line at the teaching job fair to speak with a representative from a large school district in the Denver area. I was engaged full throttle in the job search, and I was pretty sure this job fair would yield the golden ticket. My goal was to teach in the Denver area, where I could still be fairly close to my hometown of Casper, Wyoming, and in the backyard of my beloved Denver Broncos. I had gotten interviews with six school districts, and I was trying to make it a lucky seven—seven interviews, the number seven, John Elway, the Denver Broncos, teaching in Denver. Everything seemed to be falling into place. But as I was standing in line, I glanced at a poster for another school district matching the folder my mom had handed me a few weeks earlier. I dug through my backpack to confirm my hunch, and sure enough, there at the bottom of the pile was a folder identical to the poster hanging above my head. Craning my neck, I looked at the long line ahead of me. Perhaps fate was once again calling toward the shore, beckoning me toward Texas, and presenting another reminder that this school district and I were meant to be together. Giving up my place in the queue, I scooched out of line and stepped up to the empty booth.

The man sitting behind the booth stood up and introduced himself. He proceeded to tell me a little about the school district, information I had already heard from my mother, and he asked me to tell him a little about myself. There was one remaining interview slot open for the next day, and he wondered if I was interested in coming back to talk with him some more. Despite the interview being at eight o'clock in the morning, I agreed, shook hands, and walked back to where I was staying for the evening. I never got back in the other line.

Without giving too many boring details about the interview, I will say that the man behind the booth was the same man who met my mom on the tram in Dallas. He told me he might contact me in a couple of weeks to follow up, which he did. He then flew me to Grapevine to interview with twelve different principals, in *one* day no less. The weekend concluded with him offering me a job, which I accepted.

Perhaps this is why Sierpinski's Gasket resonated so deeply with me. Each of these points in my life, if observed in isolation, seemed random. I mean, do any of us really consider the bigger purpose in life when we get on a tram or start up a conversation with someone we assume we'll never see again? Instead of taking the job at the preschool that first year of college, I could have gotten a job at the local paint store where I'd dropped off an application. I may have decided I was too busy to drive to see my friend in Colorado. My mom or uncle could have stopped to get a drink or tie a shoe and sat on a different tram with different people.

This seems to be how life goes for most of us. Each choice, every decision, all of our near misses and lucky breaks accumulate as dots being laid down in the Sierpinski's Gasket, tracks in the snow, as we make our way through life. For some of us, the tracks may appear to be ordered and predictable, like a deer trudging along a well-worn path as he toils for daily sustenance. For others, the tracks look random and scattered, as if they were created by children or a puppy playing in fresh snowfall before the sun's rays or earth's winds take it away. No matter what pattern the dots end up making, we can choose to look back on chapters of our life, or the entire volume, and see the rhythm, prose, and themes from our story. We see how one event or decision led to another event or decision, and even though we did not sit down and plan out, or get to choose, every detail of our lives at the beginning of the journey, it still has a unique form, structure, and truth. And if you look closely between the dots, you start to see signs of mercy, redemption, and grace propelling you forward all along.

I remember leaving school once after a long day of teaching, and I stopped by the grocery store on my way home. As I was checking out, the cashier asked, "You're a teacher, aren't you?"

I looked up from my wallet and tilted my head to peer at this clairvoyant standing before me. I let out a breathy snort of a laugh as I answered, "How did you know that? Have you seen me at the school?"

"No, I can always recognize the teachers when they come through the line."

My snort was now a chuckle. "Why, because we're so exhausted and beat down?"

"No, you always have chalk on your clothes and marker on your hand."

Her index finger navigated along the side of her other hand, from the tip of her pinky to her wrist. I looked at that spot on my own hand and could see a blue tattoo from the Vis-à-Vis marker I used as I annotated slides on the overhead projector.

In my early years as a teacher, chalk dust was evidence of my work throughout the day. Proof of grace, doing a job I was not fully prepared to do; evidence of mercy, making it through each day with just enough energy to turn around and do it all again tomorrow. Even though blackboards have now been replaced by dry erase markers and interactive whiteboards, I still see traces of chalk dust covering my life. It's the reflections from stories of a time gone by. A time when teaching was a struggle, when I would wake up in the middle of the night ruminating over everything gone wrong during the day. A time when everything seemed to be in short supply, from money to friends to confidence. A time when each day brought new experiences, insights, and a chance to grow. A time when I was sustained by the penetrating power of kindness and generosity from others.

A little less than five years after taking a job washing dishes at a preschool, I moved to Texas to start my teaching career. What seemed like chaos—aimless and arbitrary events strung together—was finally taking shape. Let the chaos game begin.

## CHAPTER 1 *The Box*

I WALKED INTO MY VERY FIRST CLASSROOM for the very first time holding nothing but a box. My mom had been stuffing a few items inside this box now and then for a few months, leading up to me starting my first teaching job after college. She took all the sports pennants off my bedroom wall and put them in there, along with some school supplies, an old Cub Scout activity book, and a few classroom decorations she found on clearance during the summer. The box wasn't even full.

I drove into the parking lot of the school exhausted after a full day of orientation meetings for new teachers. A new coworker, whom I met in the very last session of new teacher orientation, introduced herself as Mary and asked if I would like to follow her to the school after the meeting was over. She was going to pick up her room key and drop some supplies off in the classroom. Honestly, I did not want to follow her to the school and get my room key, but she was trying to be helpful and I didn't want to come across as rude. I was reluctant because I knew once I stepped into my classroom, I would have hours of work to get my classroom ready for children. My original plan was to go home and come back early the next day to get started. Not wanting to explain any of this to my new colleague, I smiled, thanked Mary for the offer, and followed her to the school.

I had seen the school once before when I came to Grapevine for my job interview. The Director of HR, Mike, picked me up at the airport and drove me around town, showing me every elementary school in the district. Each school was clean and well kept. Some were newer than others. A few of the schools sat by themselves in a neighborhood, while others were clustered together with a middle school or high school. Across the street from my school was a high school and middle school. We were like The Three Bears of schools: Papa, Mama, and Baby. I guess that made me Goldilocks; the smallest school seemed just right.

Mary and I parked and walked into the school together. I didn't know Mary's backstory, or her last name for that matter, but she and the administrative assistant sitting at the front desk already knew each other by first name, and they were familiar enough to make small talk about the meetings and what they did the previous weekend. Mary introduced me to Sandy, and Sandy proceeded to ask me a string of questions I was way too overwhelmed to answer thoroughly or enthusiastically. I did my best to be polite as she handed me my key and gave me verbal instructions on how to find my classroom. Mary and Sandy turned out to be two of the kindest people I have ever known. Helpful, supportive, friendly, and caring. Those were all traits I was going to need in spades over the next nine months.

The school was built in the late 1970s, and many of the design features from that era were on full display. Long hallways were replaced by semicircle pods, creating clusters of classrooms arranged by grade level. There were no exterior windows in the entire building, eliminating any possibility of natural light in the classrooms. My first thought was that the building looked more like a shelter from a tornado or nuclear bomb than a place designed to ignite children's imagination and creativity. The hallways were clean and unobstructed, the walls decorated with various posters and bulletin boards. A big green C was affixed to the wall outside the fourth-grade pod. C for Curby, chaos, calamity, catastrophe. I turned left into the C pod, stopped at the first door, set my box down, and fished the key out of my pocket.

After fidgeting with the lock for a moment, I opened the door to a large, dark abyss. Whatever lurked in the belly of this black beast had never seen even a hint of daylight. The room was completely encased in interior walls. I reached into the room and began feeling around the wall nearest the door for a light switch, which I was quickly able to locate. At least the position of the light switch was familiar.

Affixed above the room were six equally spaced fluorescent lights, each holding two bulbs. Like an old farm truck that hadn't been started for a while, the lights flicked and lurched for a second before stabilizing and illuminating the entire space below. The only sound was the hum of the lights churning above, low and steady. The flood of light splashed down upon an untamed landscape of desks, chairs, and other classroom furniture in need of inventory and arranging. My gaze scanned across the pile of furniture to the back wall, which was guarded by two towering sentinels on each side. To the left was a tall bookcase built into the wall, and to the right was a cabinet with doors. I assumed the latter was designed to hold personal items such as a coat, book bag, and anything else I may want to keep hidden from children. Perhaps it was big enough for me. The two ends of the structure were separated by a long countertop and cabinets, which included a small sink. The countertop was a bright yellow, and the cabinets were a hybrid avocado/lime green.

Sitting atop the gaudy countertop was another item in the room (besides the light switch) with which I had some familiarity, a Macintosh LC520 all-in-one computer. Everything else in the classroom—the desks, the walls, the unwritten lesson plans—I had never set up completely on my own before. I had the exact same computer in my apartment, and it was the nicest thing I owned next to my mountain bike. I had taken out a loan in college to purchase my computer because, as I pitched it to my parents, having a computer in my room would help me be more efficient. I worked in a restaurant, and I was continually having to either wake up early and walk to a computer lab or trudge up the steep hill late at night after one of my shifts. The truth was, and I think everyone knew this, I just wanted a computer. They had been an obsession of mine since junior high, and I was envious of the Mac one of my roommates just purchased. And sometimes you just want something because you want it, even if you have to take out a small loan to purchase it.

My mind wandered to how perfect this situation was for me. Having identical computers at home and at work would enable me to create materials or work on projects at one location, save it on a 3.5" floppy disk, and continue the work somewhere else with no issues. At the time, the Internet was still an infant and this was the closest I would get to any sort of network. For the first time since I arrived in Texas, the stars seemed to be aligning.

I set my box down on a table near the door and walked straight to the computer. The cords and ports were familiar to me, and within minutes I had it set up. I was standing on foreign soil, encased in a cacophony of data my mind was incapable of fully processing, and the song of the computer as it started up was a familiar voice calling out my name, transporting me for a moment to a place I understood. As quickly as it started, the chords faded and I was left staring at the login screen. I didn't have a username or password yet.

As I stood in front of the computer, trying to problem-solve the password dilemma, I heard a voice break the silence from the other side of the room.

"Hello."

I swung my head around to find a middle-aged woman standing in my doorway. The rest of my body awkwardly followed so I was facing her from across the room. She was dressed casually in shorts and sandals, as if she had been working in her classroom, and I suddenly felt a surge of embarrassment at the thought of being judged for the untouched state of my classroom. I was still wearing the slacks and oxford shirt from my meetings earlier in the day, yet I felt completely exposed. There was no hiding the fact I had not moved even one desk or chair, and school was starting in a few short days.

"I'm Linda. I teach across the hall."

"I'm Curby. I just got here. My classroom's a bit of a mess right now."

"Yes, it is." She looked at the box sitting on the table right next to her. "Is that all you brought?"

Is this how it was going to be? Linda and I speaking in a continuous string of short sentences, like what you would see in a 1940s crime movie where the detective asks direct questions and the thug replies with short responses?

> *"You know her?" *holds up picture**
> *"Who's askin'?"*
> *"Someone who wants to know."*
> *"Yeah, we've met."*
> *\*detective holds up paper\* "Any idea why she wrote your name on this paper."*
> *"It's a free country. She's not who you think she is."*
> *"She's dead." \*camera zooms to closeup of thug's face\**

I let out one of those nervous laughs, the kind that is way louder and animated than the situation warrants. "That? Oh yeah, that's just some stuff my mom collected for me."

"For your classroom?"

"Yes, I haven't had a chance to unpack it yet."

Unpack? How long did I think it would take? One partially-filled box of random objects to decorate an entire classroom. Kind of like me. Incomplete, spread too thin, out of place. It was clear how unprepared I was to tackle this new endeavor. I was no longer nervous and excited to start teaching. I was scared to death.

Linda and I exchanged small talk for a few minutes. Where did I go to college? Where am I from? Am I married? Have I ever been to Texas before? After a few minutes, she must have gotten the information she was looking for. Linda needed to regroup and decide on her strategy for being stuck with this rookie for a whole year. As she slowly backed out of the room, she reminded me, "If you need anything . . . *anything* . . . I'm right across the hall."

I had no idea what she was thinking at the time, but years later she confided in me exactly what had been running through her mind: *Out of all the work he had to do, the first thing he did was set up his computer?*

I rummaged through the shelves of the closet and drawers of the teacher's desk for a little while, looked at my watch, and decided to call it a day. I had a twenty-minute drive to my apartment, and I would spend the rest of the week working in my classroom to get everything ready for the first day of school. I needed to sleep.

I was back at the school early the next morning and ready to start getting the classroom set up. I picked up exactly where I left off, standing in front of the stacks of lifeless desks with no idea where to start. When I left to go home the night before, it seemed like a simple charge: arrange the desks as soon as you get to school, then start with the rest of the room. Until this moment, I had mistaken the physical act of moving desks around the classroom for the strategic placement of those desks in some sort of arrangement in which children would learn. I had actually never distinguished between the two.

I stared at my unorganized room with nothing more than a bunch of desks, a box filled with assorted objects, and a computer I couldn't log in to. I needed ideas. I needed some guidance. I needed encouragement. In other words, I needed my mom, but she wasn't there. Society was at the cusp of cell phones disrupting everything, but at this moment they were unaffordable and unnecessary for most people. Remote telecommunication with someone a thousand miles away was how they communicated on *Star Trek* or *The Jetsons*, not 1995 Grapevine, Texas. Yet here I stood, totally stranded on this alien planet with no mechanism for communicating back to the mothership.

What would my mom do in this situation? She wouldn't *be* in this situation. She always knew what to do, but she wasn't here to make things right. The clock was ticking until the moment this silent vacuum of a room would be filled with children, asking me where they were supposed to sit, where to put the tissue boxes, and when they got to use their colored pencils. How had I made it through four years of college and intense teacher training without ever considering something as simple as how to arrange the desks?

I had to clear my head, so I walked out of the classroom and into the hall. I could see the lights on in the other classrooms in my pod. I knew one of those rooms belonged to Linda, but I was not sure who the other teacher was. I peeked through the narrow window in the door and saw her sitting at a cluster of student desks writing something with a Sharpie. Before I could duck away, she looked up and saw me. Dang it! The new guy's an idiot *and* a stalker!

---

She quickly stood and came walking to the door. I waited for her to open it as I stood awkwardly in the hall. She was short with short brown hair. Her smile was friendly and welcoming as she extended her hand toward me. "Hi, I'm Carol. You must be Curby. I heard you open your door a few minutes ago. Linda called me last night to tell me you were finally here."

Finally here? Had they been wondering if I would show up? I had never once considered my arrival to Timberline as something to be anticipated by anyone. Was I late? Should I have been here earlier? Did I miss something?

I glanced around Carol to see her immaculate classroom, confirming my status as a neophyte. The desks were arranged in clusters of four or five, and on each desk was a nameplate and a stack of books, both workbooks and textbooks. Every square foot of each wall was decorated with something. What, I didn't know, but it was neat and tidy and purposeful and perfect in every way. I was teaching with Mary Poppins.

Over the next couple of days, I would discover Carol and Linda had both taught more than thirty years each. They had started teaching before I was born, before my parents had even met each other. They had been around to see every educational trend and swing of the pendulum, from film projectors to VHS players, phonics to Whole Language, and back again.

Linda and Carol gave me some pointers on setting up my classroom, let me borrow a screwdriver to make all the desks the same height, and showed me some different ideas for decorating the walls. They showed me where to find some supplies for my desk, like a stapler, pens, sticky notes, pads of paper. I spent the next ten hours toiling in my windowless cave, and it eventually started to look like a place for learning. When I left the building for the day, it was dark and my car sat alone in the parking lot.

Early the next morning, Linda came into my classroom shortly after I had arrived and told me to come with her.

"Let's go. We're going to the teacher supply store to get you some items for your classroom."

"Really? They have teacher supply stores?"

"Yes, and I have a gift certificate I am never going to use, so let's go before the rush hits."

Over the next couple of hours, Linda walked me through the store, delivering a walking lecture, highlighting which items were necessary, what might be nice but I could live without, and which items were a total waste of money. She showed me a variety of posters, charts with cursive letters, and every kind of bulletin board border you could imagine. There were colorful packages of math manipulatives: little plastic dinosaurs and teddy bears, base ten blocks, and fraction sets. In one aisle stood rows of globes and maps, and one whole section of the store was nothing but workbooks in every subject area and grade level. For a young, naive teacher, this was perhaps the most overwhelming and welcome sight my eyes had seen in months.

Linda and I walked to the front and checked out. The person running the cash register scanned each item and placed them in bags. When the total of my purchases exceeded the amount of Linda's gift certificate, she paid the difference without hesitation. Though I had never been to jail before, I think I was able to experience what it must feel like when someone bails you out.

As someone who had always prided himself on being self-reliant and independent, I was starting to understand how much I needed other people. If I was going to survive this coming school year, I was going to have to lean on the two people who began working at the school since before I was born. Carol and Linda became my anchor throughout my first year of teaching. They gave me help when I asked for it but let me figure some things out on my own. They listened to me process negative emotions without telling me how I should feel, they laughed at my jokes and funny stories, and most importantly, they never made me feel inadequate or stupid. It's funny how the traits associated with being a good teacher are the same acts of kindness a teacher needs to thrive in this profession. If I could find a way to box up every kind of support a new teacher is going to need and sell it, I would make millions of dollars. Then, I could round up every first-year teacher, take them to the teaching supply store, and buy them whatever they needed.

CHAPTER 2 *Alone*

I STOOD AT THE BOTTOM OF THE STAIRS, wondering what would happen once I crossed the threshold into my new life. Each step brought me closer to the faded maroon door of the apartment for which, just minutes earlier, I had signed a year-long lease. I fidgeted with the key until the doorknob gave way and twisted to the left. I took a deep breath and stepped inside. In the movies, the onset of the protagonist's journey is heralded by a dramatic score. Mine was the sound of my sneakers squeaking on the linoleum.

This was in the fall of 1995, and I had just graduated from college in Utah. The number one song on the radio was "Waterfalls" by TLC, and the number two movie in theaters was *Dangerous Minds*, a story about an ex-Marine who teaches English in one of the toughest schools in Los Angeles. The minds I would be shaping were not as dangerous as those Michelle Pfeiffer had to deal with, but this was my first solo adventure as a young adult. I had never lived in Texas before, but I had spent every summer on a farm east of Dallas where my grandparents lived. A few months prior, I was finishing my coursework and applying for teaching jobs as I soaked up the last memories with my college friends. I wasn't exactly overwhelmed with job offers, but I had a few options, and the fourth-grade position at Timberline Elementary in the Grapevine-Colleyville Independent School

District seemed like the best opportunity. It was well-funded and thriving, the exact opposite of the setting in the Pfeiffer flick, and I considered it to be a safe place to start my teaching career.

I spent the better part of my last year of college looking for solitude. After three years of living in a fraternity house, the sound of voices, footsteps, doors opening and closing, blaring music, and the pop-pop-pop of the foosball table had all become inescapable clutter in my head, from which the only reprieve was the canyon north of campus where I would often sneak away on my mountain bike. My quest was small moments, stolen minutes here and there, when I could recharge and reflect, dream and plan in silence. An introvert trapped in an extrovert's world. As I got closer to graduation, I dreamed of having my own place, free of distractions and temptations. Within those flashes of solitude, I looked forward to the silence and stillness I had coveted for the last four years.

Memories can be tricky, and they are almost always self-serving. I can remember in detail my desire for solitude, yet the details are foggy when it comes to recalling times when I may have contributed to the noise in my house. Did I stare longingly out the front window in the living room wishing I could be left alone? Absolutely. Were there times when others needed to study or wanted to hear the movie dialogue, and I was the one playing foosball or blaring music or singing show tunes in the kitchen? Perhaps, but specific instances of any of these things are hard to recollect. There may be someone reading this who lived in this house with me, and they might remember me as the noisy one from whom they often needed a break. A more accurate description of this time in my life would be to say I loved my living situation, but I was ready to move on. I loved my friends, but I was tired of being around them all day, every day. I was ready to launch into the world on my own.

The solitude I had been craving toward the end of my days as a fraternity man came in the form of this second-floor apartment where I was standing. The flat consisted of a small galley kitchen overlooking a modest living room. The benefit of being on the top floor meant I had vaulted ceilings and even less noise than a ground floor unit. My apartment was on the back side of the building, away from the parking lot and swimming pool, by far the busiest areas of the complex. Just off the main living area was a small bathroom and a sizable bedroom. It was small, but it was all mine, and more importantly to me at the time, it was quiet. The walls were clean and freshly painted, compared to the scuffs, nail holes, and chipped paint in my fraternity house. The kitchen smelled like Ajax and Pine-Sol, and the fridge was free of spilled orange juice and moldy leftovers. The carpet looked as if it had been recently shampooed, which seemed unfathomable in contrast to . . . I tried not to think about the carpet in my fraternity house. I hadn't lived in a place this clean since I lived at home with my parents. After unloading the few belongings I had in my truck, I turned down the AC, stretched out on the floor, and took a nap.

I eventually got some furniture, a scratchy burlap couch and loveseat my aunt and uncle gave me. It had belonged to my cousin when she was in college, and now I knew why she was so eager to pass it on to me. I wouldn't acquire a hand-me-down TV for another couple of weeks, but I had a Macintosh LC520 computer and a 14K dialup modem, which gave me access to America Online. In lieu of television programs and movies, I had access to (what I thought was) an endless pipeline of information. I mainly used it to read and send emails to my family and college friends. Every day, I would hike the stairs to my apartment, set my bag down, and turn on my computer. After typing my username and password, I would initiate what was known as a "flash session," where AOL would fetch my email, then log me off. This ensured that I would not exceed the number of online hours included in my plan each month. I would linger at the door long enough to hear AOL signal its trademark phrase: "Welcome. You've got mail!" before walking across the large, wooded lot to check my physical mailbox. By the time I got back, my electronic mail would be waiting for me. Other than the occasional phone call from my parents or friends, more often than not the emails I got every day after returning from work were the only contact I had with my old life outside of Texas.

For the first time in my life, I was all alone. No one would come and go from my apartment while I was at work. The empty flat I left each morning would be waiting for me when I returned, untouched.

This is another instance of my memory not telling me the whole story. Many nights I came home tired and went to bed before nine.

I would often bring work home with me, and I would grade papers while I watched *Friends, Seinfeld,* or a baseball game on the old TV my uncle gave me. I had laundry to take care of, I cooked meals for myself, and I spent a lot of time on the phone with friends and family. I even ventured out occasionally to places where I might meet other people in my same stage of life. I was able to keep myself distracted enough not to dwell on my isolation too much, but over time I began to miss the daily interactions with my friends more and more. For some reason, my memories tend to settle on a few particular instances of extreme loneliness, but I am pretty sure it did not characterize my daily experience.

Once the school year was underway, the weekends were the hardest time to be alone. Most of the other teachers in my school would head home on Fridays by 3:30, which meant I was typically the last person in the building when I left. No goodbyes or see-yas or have-a-good-weekend. Just me leaving an empty, quiet building and walking to my car for a twenty-minute commute to my silent apartment. My friends from college were attending football games and parties, or they might be camping or meeting up for a bike ride. It was hard going from the hustle and bustle of fraternity life to having to work at meeting new people. Whatever level of loneliness I was feeling was met in equal measure by the laziness and complacency that came from having a built-in social network in my fraternity.

Teaching is exhausting, so I would usually start the weekend with a nap on my burlap couch. This helped offset the isolation I would soon start to experience. Whether I went to the grocery store or stopped by some fast-food restaurant to grab dinner or went to a movie, my loneliness followed me. I had never lived in a large metropolitan area before, and I continually reflected on the irony of the positive correlation between the number of strangers surrounding me and the intensity of my loneliness. I remember reading *Rime of the Ancient Mariner* in high school, and Coleridge's famous phrase often came to mind. "Water, water, everywhere . . ." I know, I know, you don't have to remind me, Samuel. There are people everywhere, all doing their own thing, places to go, commitments to keep, miles to go before they sleep.

As soon as I stepped into my apartment, the hum from the freeway faded away. The solitude haunted me all weekend, reminding me how irritated I would get, just months before, when people interrupted my reading or studying or contemplating as I looked out our front window at the Wellsville Mountains. Looking back, loneliness may just be the way I remember the stark contrast between living with so many guys and living alone in a new place.

My emotions were concurrently sadness and disillusionment about my current circumstances, compounded by guilt and regret from having not cherished time with my college friends more when I was able to see them every day. At times, I would have done anything to go back and sit on the threadbare couches of my fraternity house for just one evening, flip through the channels in our TV room, and talk for hours about nothing of importance. The subject matter was meaningless in most cases. The meaning in those conversations was derived from being present with each other, revealing small pieces of ourselves, and leaving the room a little more bonded than when we sat down. The weekends when I stayed home, with long stretches of time to myself, were the hardest to deal with. Deep down, I knew I would make friends eventually, but spending so much time by myself was a hard adjustment.

As socially isolated as I felt, I had family within driving distance—my grandparents, aunts, uncles, and cousins—whom I could go see when our schedules matched up. Even though this did not completely alleviate the loneliness I felt throughout the week, it provided an outlet to help mitigate those feelings. I was able to drive over for birthday celebrations, youth sports events, and camping trips with people who had loved me my entire life despite my quirks. I was fortunate to have family close enough to address the feeling of being out on my own.

Learning to be alone was probably the first adult lesson I learned after college. Life up to this point was built around groups of people. Sports teams, theatre productions, choirs, youth groups, fraternities, classes, college majors, cohorts. Until I moved to Texas, I had never been in a situation where it was up to me to get out there and meet new friends. Even the workplace was tricky, because everyone was in such different stages of life. They went home to families, to children, and sometimes even to parents for whom they were the primary caregiver. It wasn't fun, but I knew this stage in life would be temporary. If there was a manual or playbook with instructions on how to become a grownup, I would be sure to include a section on spending time alone. It was temporary, but I wasn't prepared for it.

# CHAPTER 3 *Place*

AS I FRANTICALLY SCRAMBLED to get my classroom set up for the first day of school, one of my new colleagues gave me a piece of advice. She explained, "It doesn't really matter what your room looks like when the children arrive, just make sure you have a desk for every child. You can always change them later, but the first thing every kid looks for is their desk."

She was right.

It was a Tuesday afternoon, and the students were here to drop off their supplies and meet the teacher. The children were loaded down with all of their school supplies, stretching their backpacks nearly to the breaking point. I heard the first two students coming toward the room before they even reached the threshold of the door. They were both boys, next-door neighbors, and best friends. They screeched into the room, looked at me, looked at each other, then back at me.

"Sorry we're out of breath, Mr. Alexander. When we saw your name on that list, we ran down here as fast as we could. We had to see if it was true. And it is! We actually have a boy teacher!"

"It's nice to meet you guys. Welcome to my classroom. You can put your boxes of Kleenex over th . . ."

They had stopped listening as they paced among the table groups looking for their name on one of the desks. The room was small with only twenty-one desks, so it didn't take long. They quickly evaluated their proximity to each other, judged it as acceptable, and immediately began transferring the contents of their backpacks into the desks.

One by one, this scenario unfolded with slight variations for the next two hours. The air in the room pulsated with both nervous energy and excitement. Some students burst in and looked for their desk right away. Some students stayed close to their parents, tucked in for safety as they entered the room, while others flew right past me toward their friends with not so much as an acknowledgement. Some students sized me up, cautiously judging my every word and mannerisms, while others' eyes innocently revealed their trust in me as their teacher. Some students talked directly to me, asking questions and telling me about themselves; others didn't say a word as their parents did all the talking.

By the time Meet the Teacher was over, almost every desk in the room was occupied by a unique individual. At least for the time being, every student had found their place.

I stayed at school for a couple of hours to get organized then drove to my apartment to sleep before the first day of school. As I stood in front of the mirror brushing my teeth, I thought about my place in all of this.

At that exact moment, I was standing at 32°50'27.3"N, 97°08'44.8"W, if someone wanted to find me on a map. This was a far cry, in just about every way, from 41°44'43.1"N, 111°48'58.3"W, where I would have been going through my bedtime routine just a few months earlier. At 42°48'40.7"N, 106°21'06.2"W, approximately 1,149 miles from my bathroom, my parents were an hour behind me probably debating whether to call and wish me luck on my first day or leave me alone so I could get some rest. If I left at just that second and only stopped for gas and coffee, I could probably be at their house in time for lunch the next day.

Places on the globe, each one, but also places in my heart. Pins on a map, but also dog-eared pages in my story. Other than perhaps the very first fraternity party I ever attended, I had never felt so out of place in my entire life. In just a few hours I would be standing at 32°54'49.1"N, 97°06'59.8"W, another dot on a map, and on that Wednesday morning when the minute hand was somewhere near the twenty-five and the hour hand was slightly past the seven moving toward eight, I would start my life as a teacher.

The first few days of school seemed to revolve around the concept of place. This is how you organize your three-ring binder. Make sure there is a place for every subject. Math goes in the yellow folder, science is green. I don't know why social studies is red, maybe it should be blue. No, we're in Texas, definitely red. Don't just shove all your papers inside your desk. They need to be in their proper place, which is why we have a folder for each subject. That crate over there is where you put your writing journals, and the space below it is where we will store the math supplies. That empty corner in the back of the room will be our classroom library as soon as I get some books. The area right behind where I am standing is my desk. That's my place. We also have a place for eating lunch and for playing at recess and for different kinds of classes. Sometimes we will go to the computer lab, other times the library. Okay, it's time for music. Does anyone know where the music room is? I could use some help here. A place for everything, everyone, at every moment of the day.

I tried to find ways to let the students personalize their own place. Each child created a nameplate to replace the one I used to indicate where they should sit on the first day. I encouraged them to turn each letter of their name into a picture that represented something about them. The letter "o" could be a soccer ball or the sun or the wheel of a bike. An "m" could be mountains or a mansion or a mangrove tree. The children enthusiastically decorated their names to symbolize their lives or the life they hoped for or maybe just the life they wished could be true.

The desks were organized into clusters of four or five, and I let each pod give themselves a name. Some teams quickly reached consensus and began working on the poster that would eventually hang above their heads. One group in particular consisted of one child with a strong opinion about their team's name and three students who really didn't care at all, or at least they didn't want to expend the energy for group processing. A few other groups argued furiously over names, some eventually gave up and agreed to a mascot they hated. Their only consolation seemed to be in the fact they would be changing desks in about six weeks, so being labeled as a panda or unicorn appeared to be more of a nuisance than a life sentence.

After a couple of weeks of teaching, my main job appeared to be telling children where everything was supposed to go. I had never thought about it before, but just about everything I taught had a place in the curriculum, and everything in the curriculum had its place. The question was not so much, "What do you think?" but more "Where does this go?"

In math, I taught the children how to line up *decimals* for addition and subtraction, but to line up *numbers* for multiplication. If they were dividing, don't forget to move the decimal from here to here. Now make sure you line up those numbers right there because if they are not in the right place, you will get the wrong answer. This is the numerator, so it goes on top. The denominator goes on the bottom. Remember, "d" is for denominator and "n" is for numerator, and "new grass grows on top of dirt." If we have the coordinate pair (3, -5), you put the dot here. If you switch the numbers to (-5, 3), the dot goes up here. The coordinates tell you where to place the dot. I have no idea when you will use this in real life, but you have to know it for the test, so don't forget. Here, let's practice a few more times. The coordinates determine the place, or is it the other way around? What if I want to just pick a place then figure out the coordinates once I get there?

Okay, let's move on to writing. You start in the upper left corner of the paper and write from left to right. Don't forget to leave a margin around the edge of the paper. Don't forget to leave some margin in your life, as well. You need to leave some space for your thoughts to wander from time to time. If you take a step back from your own story, unless you space out your words and keep it all lined up, it will look like a jumbled mess. Space, alignment, structure, order, margin, and place. Now, if you are writing this kind of sentence, the comma goes here, but not always. Sometimes it goes there. Sometimes you have to use a comma, and other times you get to decide whether or not to include it. There's a rule for this but not for that. The same is not always true for periods. If there is supposed to be a period, you better put one, otherwise it might change the meaning of the sentence. You will think you are saying one thing, but the reader is hearing something else entirely. Quotation marks, apostrophes, colons, semicolons, ending punctuation, they all have their place. When you need them, they better be there. The same goes for spelling.

Sometimes you place the "i" before the "e" and other times you switch it. If you put these two letters together you get this sound, and some words sound exactly the same even when they are spelled differently. If you place this word in your sentence it changes the meaning entirely. The same is true for capital letters and punctuation, so pay attention to where everything goes.

You will need to know why some animals are able to live here and others thrive there, and why this group of people settled here but another civilization sprung up there. What causes some groups of people to sometimes fight over a place for hundreds of years, while different groups of people coexist in peace? What are the barriers that separate us and the channels that connect us? This creature eats only plants and doesn't pose a threat to anyone, but it's a food source for bigger, more aggressive predators. Where is our place in this chain of life? Where is our place in a system into which we are inherently embedded yet equally able to understand and analyze? We live on this planet and depend on everything it provides, but we are the only creatures here who even attempt to make sense of our place in the world. Do we use our knowledge to preserve and protect the world around us, or do we exploit it for personal gain? We know our place on the map and in the timeline, and we have learned those facts about other people. Does it cause us to understand them more, to honor their story, or do we continue to be afraid of each other, skeptical of anything that is different, scared of the "other"?

And at the end of it all, where does it leave you? Once you take all the notes and pass all the exams, after you write all the papers and complete the projects, what have you learned? You may know where everything goes—commas, periods, numbers, creatures, people. Now what? Where does all of this information leave you? Where do you go from here?

Even the curriculum, a series of objectives and progressions, had its place in this stage of each child's education. If I didn't make sure they learned all of this material before they left fourth grade, there was no way I could expect them to be prepared for new challenges in fifth grade. How could I expect them to be prepared for middle school if they weren't successful in elementary school? I had no control over what happened before they came to me, but I could control, or at least try to influence, the 180 days they were in my class. One hundred and eighty days. Not even a full year. They were in my classroom less than eight hours a day. Not even a full day. Even in their nine or ten years on this planet, their time with me was barely a blip on the radar. They came in and found their desks, and just when I thought I was finally getting warmed up, they were packing up and heading off to the next grade. Some days as a teacher seemed to grind along too slow for human perception, but 180 days just doesn't seem like enough time to make a difference. Will my students leave my classroom in a better place—academically, interpersonally, existentially—than when they arrived?

## CHAPTER 4 *In Loco Parentis*

LOOKING BACK, I DIDN'T INTERACT with most of my students' parents on a daily, or even weekly, basis. Some parents I saw nearly every day because they spent so much time volunteering at the school. Others I would see about once a week or so, mostly at drop-off or pickup from school. Those interactions were typically cordial and friendly, involving a greeting and occasional small talk. There were always those parents I only saw once or twice the entire year, such as at Meet the Teacher, Open House, or a parent teacher conference. Even more baffling was that small subset of parents or guardians whom I never met, not even one time, despite my efforts at scheduling meetings or inviting them to school events. This was rare and always made me sad.

The parents whose children I taught came in all shapes and sizes, displaying all sorts of parenting behaviors. Some were strict, others were permissive. Some were engaged and involved, others were detached and distant. Some parents had flexible jobs and could attend just about every school event. Some worked all the time and were hardly ever home. The only constant I could find when it came to working with parents was that there was no ubiquitous formula explaining their availability or parenting choices.

Besides the fact that Grapevine was a suburb nestled among a massive metroplex and Casper, Wyoming, sat as an island on the plains, the two communities were surprisingly similar. The majority of my students and their families looked like me, went to churches similar to mine, enjoyed the same sports that I did, and seemed to place education as a high priority. They told their children to listen to their teacher, to do their homework, and to get along with their classmates.

Grapevine was more racially diverse than where I had grown up, but at the time I was living there it was not nearly as eclectic as other parts of the DFW metroplex. I had students from just about every racial and ethnic background. Some of them spoke other languages at home, and occasionally I would have a student who was still learning to speak English. This was a stark contrast to Casper, where the primary type of diversity was in socioeconomic status.

Just like most of my students, I was from a middle-class family. Both of my parents had post-graduate degrees and worked at the local college. Casper's economy was mostly based on the oil and ranching industries, so many of my friends' parents worked hourly jobs involving manual labor. My parents had the entire summer off so we could take long trips to visit my grandparents in Texas and Louisiana while most of my friends hung around their neighborhood and created their own fun. Some of my friends thought I was from a rich family, but I knew that was not the case.

Compared to Casper, Grapevine felt like an affluent town. The homes that fed into my school were expensive, the parents worked good jobs, and some of the families only had one parent who worked. I didn't necessarily feel out of place, but I couldn't relate to the beach and ski vacations some of my students took over the holidays. Most of my vacations involved visiting family, which was also true of some of the other families in my class.

It's hard to explain where I fit within this new community and how it compared to my experiences as a child. It was a like a giant Venn diagram, where the families and I had clear differences, but there was a large area between our two circles that overlapped, representing what we shared. One thing I knew we all had in common was the children. No matter the background, the income, the amount of education, or the languages we spoke at home, we all wanted the best for the children in my fourth-grade class. We could all come up with examples for times when we put their needs and interests before our own, which was the common ground uniting us all.

Teaching gave me a front row seat to the deep and complex relationship parents have with their children. My students made their own choices, yet their character and behavior was not shaped in a vacuum. They were the product of an intricate social and emotional ecosystem years in the making. For this reason, my students' parents often found themselves in the position of explaining, condemning, personalizing, disapproving, justifying, and excusing their children's choices all at once. Parents were caught in this dialectical tension of both protecting their children and preparing to launch them into the world. As a young teacher, I did not have a parent's perspective on any of this. Rather than seeing students as a work in progress, I tended to view their behavior as an end product through the lens of how it directly affected me as a teacher. Through many formative experiences, I learned how problematic this perspective could be.

My first confrontation with a parent involved Hunter, who would leave his three-ring binder at home every single day. No joke. Each day the students would come in, put their homework in the slot labeled with their name, then start working on the "bell ringer": a collection of redundant daily tasks to complete each day during the first few minutes of school. As if on cue, Hunter would walk up to me on the brink of tears and tell me he left his binder at home. Befuddled, I would silently ask myself, "How does one forget their binder at home every single day?" Yet, every single day I would let Hunter go to the office and call his mom, who gladly brought the binder to school without fail. Maybe she liked being needed, or perhaps she was just as forgetful as he was and didn't mind making an extra trip to the school every morning. Rather than take the time to address this daily annoyance, considering the bigger issues I was dealing with, I allowed this ritual of forgetting and being bailed out to continue, and it became just another part of my day.

The next year, I was talking with a fifth-grade teacher who had Hunter in her class, and I asked her, "So, does he still forget his binder every day?" My colleague coolly explained how he forgot it one time and she let him call his mom. Then he left it at home again the next day, and she told him he would just have to go without it for the day and his homework would be counted late. Hunter's mom showed up at her door angry and full of excuses, but my veteran colleague didn't budge. She said they had a productive conversation about responsibility and how fifth grade is the last chance Hunter will have to develop good habits before going to middle school, and he never left his binder at home again.

My colleague didn't say it, but I knew what she was suggesting: I was just as much a part of the problem as Hunter and his mom. It just seemed easier to dodge the potential thunderstorm of conflict with his mom by letting him call. Besides, she was one of the few parents who was nice to me, and she would flatter me with effusive praise for being understanding and patient with Hunter. In the process, I left him out in the rain to get drenched in his own bad habits.

This was when I realized children and their parents were not variables in my equation; I was a variable in theirs. They started this process before I was part of the story, and it would continue long after my chapter was over. I was in a temporary partnership with each parent, helping them prepare their child for the future. Sometimes the collaboration was impaired by the parent's need to be wanted or needed by their children, or their desire to slow down time and keep their children from growing up too fast. Other parents were dealing with their own issues, a hurtful past or destructive habits, and had a hard time making space for their children as they dealt with their own wounds. There were parents whose struggle to provide for their children was the main factor keeping them separated. Long hours at work, extra shifts, second and sometimes third jobs on the weekends. This dilemma thrust upon working parents by society seemed cruel, cold, and unjust.

I always felt a little guilty calling parents about their child's misdeeds. It felt a little like tattling or following through on a threat. On one hand, parents needed to know what was happening at school, but I also tried to imagine what it would feel like if the only time I heard from the school was when my child was sick or in trouble. Every parent probably needs some affirmation that others see good in their child.

I tried to handle things myself in the classroom as much as possible. I would start with reminders: "Please sit down," "I need you to work quietly so others are not distracted," or "Leaving your homework at your house is becoming a pattern." When those gentle—and sometimes not so gentle—nudges lost their power, then came the consequences, like losing recess or other privileges, even though I knew deep down this was a kid who desperately needed a break, a chance to run around for a few minutes and play with friends. Despite my best efforts at creating an orderly learning environment, structure, and high expectations, there were times when the last resort was to get a child's parents involved. I was able to deflect this confrontation with Hunter's parents, for the most part, but I would soon discover that when it came to parent-teacher interactions, I had a lot to learn.

## CHAPTER 5 *Fuzzy*

THE CIRCUMSTANCES LEADING TO MISTER JOINING our family are still not clear to me. I was home from college visiting my family over a long weekend, and our cat Abby was fixated on something under the refrigerator in our kitchen. For three days, our cat pawed at the space between the floor of the kitchen and the bottom of the fridge. She would lay on her side and slide her front paw as far as it would reach. She would then swipe her arm back and forth, reaching for the mystery object. At one point, I used a yardstick to see if I could retrieve the object our cat had obviously lodged just beyond her reach. My efforts had the same result as Abby's, and I just assumed she was being her young and playful self. Unlike the cat, I walked out of the kitchen and didn't think again about the space beneath the fridge until my dad mentioned it to me on the phone after I arrived back on campus and I was able to picture the scene in my mind.

It turns out the reason Abby was so focused on the fridge was because a baby rat was underneath, hiding from her and our dog, Buffy. Honestly, the cat would have been much more problematic for the rat, and the dog did not seem to be bothered, or aware, of his presence in the kitchen. Our dog had never hunted, much less killed, another living creature in her life, and the rat had very little to be concerned about. I asked my dad if they ever had problems with rodents in the past, and he said no. What made this particular rat so mysterious was that it was the type one would buy in the pet store or find in some sort of lab so you could run experiments to see how much Diet Coke he could consume before growing an extra nipple. This wasn't the kind of rat you find wandering in the sewer or river. A rat like this would not be likely to survive very long in the wild, which is why my sister decided to keep him as a pet. She named him Mister.

At the exact same time my family discovered Mister, one of my college roommates, Dave, discovered two rats in our fraternity house almost identical to Mister in size and color. These were not the kind of rats Indiana Jones encountered beneath the library in Venice at the outset of his Last Crusade. No, they were the type of rats you buy to feed your pet ball python. I asked Dave where they came from, and he didn't know. He was just lying on his bed listening to music and noticed something moving from his peripheral vision. When he turned his head, he saw two small rodents scurrying across the carpet from my closet toward his bed. By the time I had made the eight-hour drive back to campus from my hometown, they had been captured and were living in a shoebox on my roommate's desk. He showed me the two captives, and I kindly told him they would have to find a new place to live. No rats in my room, thank you very much. I could almost bear to look at their faces, but those tails. Dear God, those tails. Not in my room. I could almost feel the rat tail gliding along my face, across my cheek, as I was sleeping. To this day, the hair on my arms stands straight up when I think about how one of those rats might have escaped the shoebox and climbed onto my face in the middle of the night.

The best we could piece together was that someone, I assume from another fraternity or sorority, bought the baby rats at the pet store and released them into our house as a prank. What could be funnier than infesting a fraternity house with baby lab rats who would eventually mate and turn feral. Real freaking hilarious. In an attempt to find shelter, or food, one of the rats must have climbed into my laundry basket, which I loaded into my car so I could do my laundry at my parents' house over the weekend. When I dumped the clothes on the floor of my parents' laundry room, it must have made a break for it, climbed the stairs, and found refuge under the fridge, just out of Abby's reach. So many plot points in this narrative seem implausible. How did a baby rat jump into my laundry basket? How did I not see it when I was sorting my laundry? How did it not get thrown into the washer and drown? I will never know the real story behind Mister's journey from Utah to Wyoming and into my sister's heart, but he was a member of the Alexander family for nearly three years. Tail and all.

Mister isn't the only reason I never pictured myself as one of those teachers with a classroom pet. I can also attribute being pet-averse to my third-grade teacher, Mr. Lyon. One would assume with a name like that his classroom would be a menagerie of all sorts of critters, and it was. He had a variety of reptiles and rodents in his classroom, but the event that sealed the deal for me was when he tried to hatch baby chicks.

One Monday, all of us entered his classroom to find an incubator sitting in the corner, a warm, glowing dome filled with eggs. Mr. Lyon explained how these eggs, unlike those we find in the grocery store and eat for breakfast, had been fertilized and would hatch in a couple of weeks. I don't recall thinking much about the fertilization process at the time, but in retrospect I imagine these eggs were the product of a clandestine barnyard affair between a rooster and a hen.

After about three weeks of waiting for the eggs to hatch, Mr. Lyon announced to the class that the eggs were duds and our experiment was not going to result in cute baby chicks. As a consolation prize, he brought in a bunch of chicks he bought from a local farmer so we could see what should have been the result of this class project. Every kid in the class got a turn to come to the box where the chicks were chirping and help them get their first drink. I gingerly picked up one of the small, yellow fluffballs and dipped its tiny beak into a small dish of water. I then placed the chick in a different box so Mr. Lyon could keep track of who had already gotten a drink. Clearly, his classroom management skills were not confined to human children.

The joy that effused throughout the classroom was quickly dimmed when we learned about the second half of Mr. Lyon's experiential lesson plan. Our teacher explained to the class he needed to learn more about the source of the failed class project. He informed us that unhatched eggs are either nonviable or infertile. If the eggs were nonviable, there was likely an issue with the embryos themselves or with the incubator environment, such as temperature, humidity, ventilation, or turning. If there were no embryos at all, the problem was probably with the reproductive systems of one or both parents. This made perfect sense to me, and I was impressed with Mr. Lyon's tenacity to see this project all the way through, even when the results were not what he was hoping for. What I did not expect was that he wanted to identify the root of the problem right then and there in the school parking lot.

The teacher called out the names of five or six students, of which I was one, who rose from their desks and followed Mr. Lyon out the door. I marched with the other students as Mr. Lyon retrieved six eggs from the incubator, only adding to the melancholia. We stood at the edge of the parking lot as Mr. Lyon tossed the eggs, one by one, onto the asphalt of the parking lot. Each smashed egg revealed a small chicken embryo, resting between a pool of yolk and bits of eggshell. My classmates and I stood in silence, staring at the massacre before us, as Mr. Lyon turned to walk back into the school and told us plainly, "Hmm, nonviable." I have never gotten this image out of my head, and it cemented within my teacher brain the belief that any class project involving animals was traumatic and nonviable, including classroom pets.

What I never predicted was inheriting a classroom pet against my will, which is what happened when I saw José, the school maintenance man, walking down the hall with two hamster cages.

"Hey, José, got a couple of buddies?"

"No, you do."

He stopped and asked me if I wanted him to drop off the hamster in my classroom, or if I wanted to take it right now. Neither, actually. I wanted him to keep walking and forget he had ever seen me.

Before I could say anything, José walked into my classroom and set one of the cages on the table nearest the door. Linda, one of my teaching partners in the fourth grade, followed us into the room and began explaining how a family in the school was moving and couldn't take the hamsters with them. *Nice move, parents*, I thought. Well played. Linda had been in the office when the pets were abandoned—I mean, donated.

She agreed right there and then to take one and give the other hamster to me. The cages came in blue and pink, presumably because the hamsters were male and female. Linda asked José to deliver the hamsters to their new homes. By color, of course. I got the blue cage.

Most people would have had no problem turning away a homeless pet. Maybe they have allergies or other pets who would try to eat a hamster. Some people have no problem just saying no and leaving it at that. I'm sure there were people in the building who, had they known my true feelings, would have taken the hamster off my hands. All I had to do was make an announcement or send a note home with my students.

Other people can't say no. They're too worried about what people might think of them. They put way too much effort into their image. They may even try to out-good others, you know, be competitively altruistic. And what could be more selfless than receiving this helpless animal with open arms? I was too new at this school to be the villain. I was "other people."

My school day ended with me staring at this animal, sizing him or her up. I never bothered to learn the basics of caring for a rodent when my sister had a rat living in our house. I couldn't tell whether it was a male or female, and I had no idea what to name an orphaned hamster. Annie? Oliver? Jane Eyre? Just the word "rodent" made me uneasy. I was already in a perpetual state of feeling behind, with never enough time to do what had to be done. Now I would have to find a place that sold hamster food and bedding. I would have to remember to feed this animal on a regular schedule and find the time to clean the cage. Were there any other requirements for keeping another living creature alive? Was food and water enough, or was there something else I needed to do? If there was some magic formula for raising a hamster, I didn't know where to find this information. No teacher wants to be remembered for accidentally killing the class pet. There are grown-ups who make a respectable living exterminating rodents from homes and office buildings. I associated them with disease and plagues and infestations. My classroom suddenly became a little more precarious.

My fourth-grade students noticed the hamster cage in the back of the room about as quickly as my classmates and I noticed the incubator in my third-grade classroom. I knew as soon as they arrived, we would not get anything done that day until we talked about the newest member of our class.

Despite my feelings about this animal, the decision to add the hamster to our classroom was for the students, so I decided to let them name him. In the spirit of democracy, the kids voted using the time-honored method of putting heads down and raising their hands. After some deliberation, the hamster was henceforth known as Fuzzy. Just like that, Fuzzy became another part of my daily routine. This routine involved checking his water and food, and changing his bedding each Friday. I would look in his cage each morning to make sure he was still there. He was.

It wasn't until one of my students finished an assignment early and asked, "Mr. Alexander, can I fill Fuzzy's water bottle since I'm done with my work?" that the epiphany came to me. These kids were nine and ten years old. If I could care for a hamster, so could they. My sister wasn't much older than these kids when her stowaway rat came into our family. They could fill his food dish, change his bedding, provide him with empty toilet paper tubes. I didn't even know why people put toilet paper tubes in hamster cages. Were they for chewing? Hiding? Plotting world domination? Who knows? What I did know was when my class pet—no, *our* class pet—got new toilet paper tubes, the students would provide them!

"Good morning, everyone, and welcome to our new class project." Now all I had to do was convince the students to take Fuzzy home on the weekends.

Children have been doing variations of this activity for years, so this wasn't a completely novel idea. Teachers would send home Flat Stanley or some sort of stuffed animal, and the children would do a project while they hosted their little inanimate guest. They could write about what they ate for dinner or did for entertainment, discuss where they slept, or what time they had to wake up in the morning before school. It was like having a little private investigator inside each student's home, giving me some insight into what their lives were like the other seventeen hours each day they weren't in my classroom. The possibilities of this project began to light up my imagination like fireworks you could see way off in the distance. Their brilliance is visible right away, but the boom would come later. In my case, much later.

I was motivated. All I had to do was create a sign-up sheet for interested students, and organize a "travel kit" for Fuzzy. I would stock it with the journal for the writing project, some food, extra bedding for when the students cleaned Fuzzy's cage, and his plastic spherical walking bubble. Was I forgetting anything? No, this just about covered it.

This project came to be known as "Fuzzy's Travels." As I fantasized about this project, I would create a template for them to follow in their journal entries, each new page would go in the book we would write for the class library. The students could make scientific observations about when Fuzzy slept and when he was awake. They could read the ingredients on his food and research which food sources from the wild it was trying to emulate. Students could even create graphs and charts to record their data. I would write a song to go with the project, and we would sing it right before each student shared their Fuzzy story, which of course would be unimaginably cute and creative because the students would love the project so much. The yet-to-be-written notes from the parents would say things like, my son refused to go to his baseball game because he couldn't stand the thought of leaving Fuzzy at home by himself. Or, as soon as my daughter finished writing her journal entry for Fuzzy's weekend at our home, she became obsessed with all the Ralph S. Mouse and Stuart Little books and she hasn't stopped reading since. This played out like a television show in my mind, maybe even a feature-length film. Engaged students, high-quality work, laughter, memories. I could write a book and include a copy of my song with it. I would be on Letterman, maybe even Oprah. Teacher of the Year, and oh, it's with a C not a K! I would be played by Matt Damon.

The next Monday, during writing time, I pitched the idea. I told the class we were going to start a project called "Fuzzy's Travels," and each student would get a turn to take Fuzzy home for a weekend. They could play with him, change his bedding and take care of him, then write about it and share their story with the class. Even as the words came out of my mouth, this did not sound as good as it looked in my imagination. One student immediately raised her hand.

"My mom hates hamsters. My brother's escaped once and ruined a pillow on our couch. We found it dead a week later under the dryer. It really stank."

I thought, *Well, your brother's cage sucked, and this one doesn't, so that won't happen. Next question.* Defensiveness is the first indication there might be holes in your plan and you are plugging them with wishful thinking.

"I'm sure this cage is pretty secure. I've had it two weeks, and Fuzzy hasn't escaped yet."

Another hand.

"Who gets to go first?"

The second flaw was exposed, and I immediately tried to fill it. "Well, I have been thinking about who gets to go first as a reward for good behavior." Oh, that was such a manipulative lie. I hadn't thought about a queuing system until that very moment. I didn't even know it was called a queuing system.

So, I would choose who gets to go first, and the rest of the class could duke it out over a sign-up sheet. I decided to cover the basics of hamster care for the next two days in science. I hadn't planned anything, but I had done this enough times to wing it. I showed them how to fill the water, change the bedding, and how to properly close the opening to the hamster ball so in case Fuzzy bumped up against something the door wouldn't fall off. I had learned that one the hard way.

An unexpected twist in this adventure was how Fuzzy was starting to grow on me. He was this small furry creature that fit in the palm of my hand. He would run up and down my arm when I held him, which oddly enough, was happening more and more often. His face was definitely the most adorable part of him, with that little snout, cute whiskers, and big brown eyes that seemed out of proportion to the rest of his face. When he ate, he would hold the food in his cute little paws and nibble at a fast pace, like something you would see in a cartoon. His bottom waddled when he walked, kind of like a toddler. Sometimes I would be grading a set of papers or putting materials together for the next day, and Fuzzy would catch my eye. I would just stop and watch him play or eat or drink for a minute, then I could get back to work. For the first time, I was starting to understand why some people were so attached to their pets.

The first Friday of my experiment rolled around, and I had everything ready to go. The extra bedding sat unopened in the travel kit, the food was closed up tight with a rubber band, and the all-important travel log was in a folder, along with some instructions on how to complete the project and care for the animal. I reminded Susan, my first volunteer, several times that she would be taking Fuzzy home with her.

Susan was by far the most responsible child in my class, and she got to sail the maiden voyage of Fuzzy's Travels. She was the oldest child in her family, and the only other sibling was a baby brother. Her parents had obviously taught her the finer details of personal responsibility, kindness, and respect. When other students in the class blurted out answers to my questions during lessons, Susan would calmly raise her hand and wait her turn. Sometimes I would call on her, even after one of her less-refined peers had shouted out the correct answer, my way of acknowledging and validating appropriate classroom behavior.

Susan was the perfect person to pilot this project because if anyone in the class was going to help it get off to the start it deserved, it was her. It was one thing to have a proper example that I created and showed the class, but when the exemplar came from a student, it was always more impactful. The students expect the teacher to know how to do something right, but when they see one of their peers achieve greatness, they are somehow motivated, if only temporarily, to be great, too.

I sent Susan out the door wearing her backpack, the bag of supplies in one hand and Fuzzy in his light blue cage in the other. I'll be honest, I did not think of Fuzzy again the entire weekend. In fact, I nearly forgot about the project until Monday morning when I saw Susan standing by my door with the bag and the cage. The fact that she was actually returning the hamster was a good sign. "How did everything go this weekend?"

"My mom wrote you a note."

When I was greeted by these words, it was rarely a thank you note or a note of appreciation or a note telling me her child suddenly loved math and couldn't wait for calculus. For teachers, this is equal to hearing, "We need to talk" from your significant other. In this context, "talk" is what the other person will be doing while you listen. Assuming a student wasn't ill the day before or about to leave on a trip, a note from a parent often meant they were annoyed enough to tell you about it but not yet mad enough to call the superintendent.

"Oh, really? Did something go wrong? Did Fuzzy escape?"

"She just said to make sure you got this note." Susan looked at me from the top of her eyes, then she looked away as I grabbed the note and stored it in my shirt pocket. Something about her body language hinted to me that this note was not thanking me for allowing the family to babysit a hamster for the weekend. She was quick to hand over the cage and bag of supplies.

I clumsily stuck my key in the lock as I held the hamster cage and bag in my other hand, and Susan opened the door. I let her lead the way into the room before reading the note. I figured, if I am in trouble, I might as well let her unpack her books and get an early start on her daily work. I set everything down and fished the note from my chest pocket. As would be expected from this family, it was in the folder with the directions and now-completed travel log. I began reading it, then glanced at Susan. She was watching intently to see my reaction. She and I both knew in that moment that if even one percent of her mom's anger had spilled onto that note, I would probably end up under my desk crying.

*Mr. Alexander,*
*Did you send home a note asking our permission for Susan to bring your hamster home for the weekend? If so, I must have missed it. In the future, please let me know when Susan will be taking care of your hamster.*

Okay, she didn't seem furious, but this was definitely a big oopsie on my part. In the midst of all my enthusiasm and eagerness to displace my responsibility for Fuzzy onto my students, I forgot one very important detail. Some parents might not appreciate having to take care of someone else's pet for a weekend, especially if it's unannounced. This also served as my first great lesson about parent-child communication. Children do not rush home and tell their parents everything, even if the news is something the parents probably want to know. So, even though Susan knew about Fuzzy's adventure at her house for a couple of weeks, she never mentioned this to her parents.

Maybe she really wanted to take the hamster home but knew her mom wouldn't let her. Or she honestly thought her mom wouldn't mind. Most likely, she forgot about it until she was walking to her mom's car holding the hamster, when she noticed the car was packed for a weekend trip to Grandma's house and she instantly put all the pieces together.

I quickly tried to think back to what my teachers would have done. Ah-ha! Permission slips! The faux pas was obvious now. As soon as I had some time that day, I put together a short form explaining the project and provided a place for the parent to check yes or no and leave a signature. I made copies while the class was in PE and sent them home that afternoon.

The next day, fifteen of the twenty-one students returned their forms. Six of the returned forms were marked no, which meant only nine students agreed to adopt Fuzzy for the weekend Another indicator of my naivete was my inability to anticipate a situation where a parent might not want a hamster in their home, such as allergies or other pets or shared custody with an ex-spouse. Once again, I was the student as I encountered another situation that broadened my worldview just a little bit more. Overall, I did not consider this to be a setback. A dozen or so Fridays of changing the bedding myself was manageable. Better yet, I could make the kids whose parents marked no clean the cage at school before they went home for the weekend. I could make it fun, like letting them clean the cage while everyone else worked on an assignment. It would be like a work release. I later backed off from this idea. As inexperienced as I was, I knew singling out students to perform manual labor was a bad idea.

I decided those six students would take home a stuffed animal and pretend he was Fuzzy. I created a schedule for the class, interspersing the stuffed and live animal kids, and sent it home with the students. I wanted to know in advance if there were any conflicts so I could make alternate plans.

The project proceeded on schedule for the next four weeks. Two of those weeks involved the hamster going home with students, and there had yet to be any problems. As I scanned my list to see who was next in line to take Fuzzy home for the weekend, I read the name out loud: Scotty.

Scotty was one of those kids who hadn't exactly had an easy life. He was born into a large family with very few resources. His household had many people crammed into a tiny rental home. He was somewhere in the middle, with older siblings in middle school and younger siblings in the lower grades. There are different approaches to parenting, most of which I had observed among my friends growing up. Some parents are patient and slow to react when their children do something wrong. They talk about issues in private, sometimes after the incident has occurred. My own parents used this from of discipline, refraining from embarrassing me in public. Other parents I've witnessed are harsh and critical and denounce their children publicly with no regard for who might be listening. In my few interactions with Scotty's mom, she came across as the latter. Even though Scotty was often the source of disruptions and frustration in my classroom, I felt sad for him when his mom called him out in front of his classmates.

An image that comes to mind was the day she stuck her head in my door and announced to me in front of a completely quiet class: "Mr. Alexander, if you see Scotty wearin' his pants with the crotch down around the knees, you call me. I ain't havin' no son of mine going around lookin' like white trash!"

"Yes, ma'am, I'll do that." I tried to move the conversation out into the hall. "Got that, Scotty? Crotch above the knee."

At this point, Scotty was pretty much trying to hide. "I told you, Mom, I ain't got no belt!"

"Then, Mr. Alexander will give you some string or something. You keep them pants up!"

I didn't mention Scotty's pants the entire day. I kept thinking, if Scotty's mom is willing to say this in front of the entire class with no hesitation, what did she say at home when no one else was around? Based on what I knew about Scotty's family, they were rough around the edges, and I wondered what Fuzzy would encounter on this visitation.

I vividly remember watching Fuzzy play the day before he went to spend the weekend with Scotty. He was running around his cage staying busy, moving things from here to there, trotting in his wheel, gnawing on a toilet paper roll, grabbing a bite to eat, and slurping a drop or two from his water bottle in between. Fuzzy had really started to grow on me. I used to avoid him, but now I greeted him each morning when I came to school, and I would usually stroll by his cage each afternoon and say goodbye before going home. His fur was soft, and there was this irresistible cuteness in his eyes and teeth. And that waddle of a walk, I could watch it all day. On Friday afternoon, after giving Scotty all the supplies and my usual rundown, I think I said a little prayer for Fuzzy.

I don't know what I was expecting on Monday, but what actually happened was not on the playlist. I knew a weekend at Scotty's house could be jarring, but something seemed to be . . . off. I couldn't put my finger on what it was. Maybe Scotty could provide more details.

"Scotty, how did things go this weekend?" I watched his every expression, analyzing even the slightest movement of his eyes.

"Oh, pretty good."

"So, everything went well with Fuzzy?"

"Yeah, yeah, it was great. We had a lot of fun with him."

Enough small talk, you little liar. I want answers. "Is there anything about this weekend you need to tell me?" Watch his eyes. Do a person's eyes dart left or right if they are lying? I can't remember! Who even came up with that theory? Just come clean and tell me! Don't make this so freaking hard! Focus.

"No, I don't think so. Why?"

"Oh, I'm just wondering. Fuzzy looks, uh, different, but I'm not sure why. Maybe he's tired or stressed out or something, and I thought you might know why."

"No, I don't know. He looks the same to me." This kid was good.

"Really? So, nothing especially eventful happened this weekend? Nothing you feel you need to tell me about? You know, Scotty, I'm your teacher and you can tell me anything. You're not in trouble, but if anything happened to Fuzzy, I *really* need to know."

"Not that I know of."

Okay, I see how it is. "Thank you for taking good care of Fuzzy, Scotty. You can go back to your desk." I'm watching you. All day, looking for a crack in this façade of lies you've created, and I'll be there when it crumbles.

---

When I was a kid, cartoons were only on TV during certain times during the day. I would watch them for thirty minutes or so in the morning before school, then again for about an hour after I got home. The morning cartoons were mainly *Looney Toons* and *Tom and Jerry*, and I watched them nearly every day throughout elementary school. It should come as no surprise that these seven-minute cartoons became a crucial piece of the cultural lens I use to filter my lived experience.

My favorite cartoons included all of the opera episodes, anything with Martin the Martian, and "Hyde and Hare." The latter, like many of the Looney Toons, was a little dark and quite a bit of the humor was lost on children. In this cartoon, Bugs Bunny gets adopted by Dr. Jekyll, a kind man who comes to the park each day to feed him carrots. For reasons not entirely explained in the narrative, Dr. Jekyll drinks "that concoction," which causes him to transform uncontrollably between the gentle doctor and the murderous green-skinned, red-eyed maniac, Mr. Hyde. The majority of the episode consists of Bugs and the doctor running all over the mansion to escape the lunatic, only to find him repeatedly—and inexplicably, from Bugs's perspective—in the exact same spot where the doctor was just standing. They run from the hallway to a barricaded room in the basement to a closet and back into the lab where the concoction started this whole disaster, and because the seven minutes is winding down the director abruptly ends the whole ordeal. The cartoon ends with Bugs walking back to his old life in the park as he transforms into a green-haired, red-eyed demon-rabbit and scares the ladies feeding the birds. This final image is what came to mind when I looked at Fuzzy.

Did Scotty give Fuzzy some sort of concoction? Has he been transforming between classroom pet and monster right under our noses? Is it possible the cycle stopped on monster, and this is the new Fuzzy? After looking at this animal from every angle, this was clearly not the same hamster who went home with Scotty on Friday. This hamster was bigger and had different markings. His fur was more course, wiry. The teeth seemed to jut out a little more than before, and there was an untrustworthy—dare I say sinister—look in his eyes. In fact, the look was not in his eyes at all. It was behind his eyes, windows into his demented soul. The most noticeable change came when I tried to reach into the cage and hold

"Fuzzy." Before my hand even reached halfway into the cage, he lunged at me. This was not an excited lunge, like when long-lost lovers reunite after the war. This lunge included bared teeth, froth, and noises akin to a snarl, just at a much higher pitch since Fuzzy was a hamster and not a pit bull. I jerked my arm back quickly, scratching my hand on the edge of the door as I quickly pulled it to safety. This was not Fuzzy, I was sure about that, and Scotty and the rest of the class knew it. This animal was clearly the result of prolonged exposure to the chaotic environment of Scotty's house, and his appearance and rabid behavior were the symptoms of hamster PTSD.

Even with this knowledge, I knew better than to drag this issue into public discussion. Scotty already had a hard time fitting in. He was always getting into trouble. He told outlandish lies no reasonable person would ever believe. His clothes were old and threadbare and hung from his pudgy body like an apparition floating through the aisles of a haunted department store. He was a misfit among his affluent suburban classmates. There were already whispers among the class about Fuzzy, and they knew something was off. If I were to voice my doubts as to who was actually occupying Fuzzy's cage, the other children would devour Scotty. He'd never make it to lunch. So, Scotty and I became silent allies, both clinging to an unspoken agreement to prop up his house of lies concerning Fuzzy's true identity. As much grief as he gave me at times, I decided in this moment to protect Scotty. Every kid in the class knew what happened. No one knew the details, but we all knew this was not the same hamster.

The new Fuzzy completely changed the class project. Students began dropping out, making excuses for why they could no longer take Fuzzy home or give him food throughout the week. The clear plastic ball sat unused, gathering dust on the shelf next to Fuzzy's cage. For the few children who understood the commitment they made to contribute to our class project at least once, I included a pair of leather gloves in the bag of Fuzzy's supplies, just in case they needed an extra layer of protection when putting food in his dish or attempting to hold him.

Fuzzy and I sat and stared at each other. I leaned back in my chair as he paced back and forth past the bars of his cage. A mirror image of this first year of teaching, my experiment with Fuzzy had not gone as planned. Nothing about this year had been as I envisioned it when I was a hopeful, idealistic college student sitting on the side of a mountain daydreaming about my first class. The Fuzzy Project, like so many of my other ill-hatched ideas, was full of flaws I failed to consider before rolling it out for students. Having my hamster switched with a body double was not on my bingo card, that's for sure.

There wasn't much I could do about this situation other than adapt to it. If there was anything endearing about the new Fuzzy, we would find it. If the parents, students, and teachers at my school could learn to accept my shortcomings, then we would certainly embrace this murine sojourner into our family. Life isn't always about who we have invited to the party. Sometimes we just have to welcome whoever walks through the door.

Welcome to my classroom, Fuzzy. I don't think we have been properly introduced. I'm your new family.

# CHAPTER 6 *Cracks*

I WAS NOT A STANDOUT IN ANY WAY AS A CHILD. I was short, moderately athletic, somewhat musically talented, and not very smart in school. I was always on the B team in basketball, I made average grades (this was when Cs were still considered a decent grade), and when girls talked about who they "liked," my name never came up. Despite being so painfully average, I had one thing on my side. I had a vivid imagination and I was a dreamer. I always assumed I would rise above my mediocrity and become something—someone—extraordinary. Elementary school fizzled out pretty much as it started, with no real accomplishments, talents, or characteristics to speak of. I was terrified for middle school.

Middle school started pretty much as elementary school had ended. The only difference was I was substantially shorter, far less athletic, and even more academically unimpressive than my peers whom I passed in the halls each day. Developmentally, I was also more prone to dwell on these differences, which meant if I was awake, I was probably thinking about it. As a last-minute change to my schedule, I dropped study hall and added choir. My prior experience with choir had been in church where my dad was the minister of music and my mom directed the children's choir. Even under these conditions, my parents were determined to never show my sister or me favoritism among our peers, and they overcompensated by making sure we blended in with everyone else. I imagine in the world of choir directing, nothing screams nepotism more than giving your own child a solo in every single performance. Besides the obvious environmental elements like water and oxygen, choir was probably the one thing I had been exposed to most in my life. It was as commonplace as taking out the trash and making sure our dog had fresh water. Perhaps this is why it took until seventh grade for me to independently select this activity from a list of alternatives, and even this was at the suggestion of my mother.

Seventh-grade choir quickly became my favorite class. At that age, no one could have convinced me to try out for a solo or do anything else that drew attention to myself, but I was aware that I was perhaps slightly better than the average child at reading my part, following direction, and singing on pitch. You don't have to be a superstar to know something like this; you only have to listen to the other singers around you. My real breakthrough came at the end of the year when my choir teacher decided to have a seventh-grade talent show in class.

When I heard about the talent show, I felt—probably for the first time in my life—an irresistible pull toward the sign-up sheet. It had been posted on the wall near the door for over a week, and the deadline to register was quickly approaching. Since this was a class talent show, there were no auditions. Rather, the teacher estimated how many acts could perform in one class period, and the first ten people to sign up were in. I walked past the sign-up sheet every day for a week, and when I noticed only two spots left, I hastily put my name down. Next to the line for your name was another line, where I had to identify my talent. This was probably a preventative measure to reduce the chance that some class clown would sign up for the talent show and proceed to jack around for three minutes. If you have to name your talent, it stands to reason you will think twice about whether or not you really want to make this kind of commitment. I took a deep breath, looked to see if anyone was standing behind me, and I scribbled down what I would be doing during my three minutes in the spotlight: breakdancing.

At this stage in my life, breakdancing was a consuming passion. I had the Adidas track suit, the boom box (it was my mom's, actually), a decent assortment of breakdance music, a sizable piece of cardboard for backspins, and my own copy of *Breakin'* on VHS tape. My best friend and I had even formed our own breakdance crew, the Pop Rockers. He went to a different middle school, so we never fully realized our potential (or dream) of battling some rival crew in the hallways of the school surrounded by the entire student body, but you can bet your unlaced Nike sneakers that we tore it up on the weekends when he was allowed to spend the night at my house. At least until midnight, of course, and only at a reasonable volume.

The choir teacher let each student perform in the order in which they signed up, and I was the second-to-last name on the list. I sat and watched each act go before me as the butterflies in my stomach became increasingly active. Since it was a choir class, most of the other performances before me were singers. They mostly sang pop songs and Broadway numbers that were easy enough for the choir teacher to sight read. A couple of students played the piano, but I was the only dancer. The person performing right before me was one of my best friends, and he struggled through the theme song from the movie *The Sting*. As he finished the final notes of his performance, I stood and carried the cassette tape with my song to the teacher while the class was still applauding, and waited for the din to subside before taking my place in the middle of the "stage." For the next three and half minutes, on a Friday afternoon during fifth period, in front of the other fifty plus members of the seventh-grade choir, I locked and popped as if the next eleven years of my life depended on it. My routine was so tight, the audience didn't know when the robot ended and the wave began. I was walking on a cloud, then moonwalking backwards, then moonwalking in a circle like an egg beater (I'm not sure if this move had a name or if I made it up). The worm became a backspin and turned into a windmill . . . well, almost a windmill. Man, I needed to practice that move more. I was in the flow, and my three minutes ended in a burst of glory that can only be described as some variation of a handspring twist that landed in the exact pose you would expect from a sheltered Wyoming kid mimicking a street-smart breaker from the Bronx. Before the music had even completely trailed off, the room erupted with the shrieks you only hear in a room full of excited seventh-grade girls (though, to be fair, the sound is indistinguishable from seventh-grade boys whose voices haven't changed yet). For the first time in my life, I had done something remarkable. My hours and days of shadowing breakdance moves in front of my TV had suddenly elevated me to a place above ordinary. No matter the outcome, I had set my eyes upon the hills and overcame fear and doubt to reach my goal. I had performed in front of a crowd doing something I loved.

It would be safe to say, this moment launched my confidence. Each success led to more confidence, which led to bigger challenges, each of which increased my success and confidence. Select choirs, solos, leading roles—I felt as if there was nothing I couldn't accomplish. I even pursued theatre during my first year of college, and my climb up the ladder of success continued. My success as a performer transitioned to academic and leadership opportunities in college. Whether it was my fraternity, my classes, or my church, there seemed to be nothing holding me back. I had friends and girlfriends, and girls who were friends who I wished would be my girlfriend. There was practically no accomplishment I perceived to be out of my reach. I perceived myself to be a rock star among my cohort of student teachers, writing songs to sing with my class, creating fun hands-on projects, and basking in the continual adoration of my second-grade students. I even got a teaching job in an amazing school district in a different state two months before I graduated. Success created more success, and the future seemed to be writing itself second by minute, hour by day.

The day I graduated from college, I stepped out of the academic palace of engineered success, and life suddenly became hard. My natural response was to feel sorry for myself.

It had never occurred to me until I began teaching full time how much work it would be or that so many of the activities I loved would have to take a backseat until I got my feet under me again. What, up to this point, had once been a fairly balanced life (though slightly tilted toward my own entertainment and recreation) was now solely focused on one thing: learning to survive in this new city and career.

Months prior, I had moved my meager assortment of belongings into a small apartment in a town next to the school district where I was teaching. The old truck I drove was paid for but needed repairs almost every month. Turning the key to the ignition each morning and afternoon, and the ensuing twenty-minute drive to and from work was a daily cocktail of stress and mystery, followed by gratitude that I made it home one more time. My first paycheck had the appearance of being big, especially when compared to every other minimum wage paycheck I had ever received in my life. Once all my bills were paid, I was able to see the truth. I was poor. I barely had enough money in my checking account to buy cereal and milk. I had no TV until my uncle gave me an old one from his attic. I had no furniture until my grandmother and aunt delivered a creaky, scratchy couch and loveseat to my apartment. I was able to buy a bed and dresser on credit and pay it off in one year with no interest. I budgeted eating at McDonald's every other week as a reward for making it to that point in the month. I had to charge some new clothes to my credit card because I had nothing in my wardrobe that would be expected of an education professional.

As if my financial situation was bad enough, I was also felt like I was pretty terrible at teaching. Was I actually terrible? I probably wasn't as bad as I thought I was, but just like in middle school, I was burdened by my own tendency to compare myself to those around me. I also felt like my students could sense my naivete upon entering my classroom for the first time, and they almost immediately pounced on it. The stream of kids asking to go to the bathroom was so steady, the hall pass rarely made it back to my desk as the students would pass it off like a relay baton.

I was new to the content and skills my students were expected to learn, and I often had to teach myself the lessons the night before I delivered them to my students. Since I did not go to school in Texas, I would read the social studies textbook every day in order to figure out the difference between Sam Houston and Stephen F. Austin, Goliad and Gonzalez. Every lesson presented a unique area of growth, and as soon as I felt like I was making progress in one area of teaching, another obstacle would surface.

My first hurdle was classroom management and trying to get the students to cooperate with me. I had made a promise to myself during college to never become one of those teachers who yells at the class. I was young and inexperienced, and I wanted the students to like me. I tried catchy incentive programs, but the students would only behave long enough to get the reward then go back to their chicanery. I tried using more punitive measures like writing names on the board or moving a clothespin to a different color on the "behavior board," but then my classroom just felt like an incessant battle of the wills. As the year progressed, I felt like I was making progress in managing the classroom, but I began to have doubts about other areas of teaching. Were the students even learning anything? The phrase "I'm confused" became so commonplace in my classroom, I eventually created little flags that students could raise every time they had a question. My intent was for students to raise the flag so they could keep working until I got to their desk. What I got was flags of surrender waving all over the room. I was in the early stages of discovering that teaching involves a complex balance of creating the environment for learning, designing lessons for learning, and using data from those lessons to make decisions about future learning. Add to the mix skills like communicating with parents and maintaining a legible grade book, and you start to see the mural of how much I was learning at once.

By the second week of school, every teacher, parent, and student in the school knew I was a tenderfoot. I would demonstrate some sign of progress, such as shifting from one lesson to the next without the entire class erupting into a cacophony of chatter, or having a whole stack of papers graded and entered into the gradebook before the next day. These small gems sat among large lumps of coal. Sometimes I would try to explain concepts to students without giving them a chance to process the information or practice. I would just blabber away minute after minute without considering whether or not the children understood any of my ramblings. Other times I would start the day off too permissive or lenient, and by the end of the day there was no amount of cracking down that would get the class back under control. I would forget to respond to a parent's note, or I might not follow up on a missing assignment until it was time to submit progress reports. That usually resulted in another note from a parent. There was no mistaking, despite four years of training, support, and guidance, there were many aspects of teaching I didn't even know I needed to learn until I was confronted by them.

This was perhaps the hardest pill to swallow. As I studied to be a teacher, I would often daydream and envision myself in my ideal classroom working with my perfect students. Not once did I ever consider I might be . . . bad at teaching. In reality, I was walking the path of every new teacher, but the constant state of learning made me focus on my incompetence rather than seeing the progress I was making each day.

After a particularly frustrating day, I called my parents for no other reason than to hear the voice of someone who I knew would love and support me no matter how awful I was at my job. We spent a few minutes updating each other on what was happening, which was really just my mom telling me some tidbits of random gossip about people in the neighborhood or at church. After we ran out of news to share, my dad brought up the topic of my teaching job. It was a simple inquiry, the kind any parent would ask their child who had just embarked on a new career. He wasn't being nosy or intrusive, and surely I should have seen the question coming.

"So, how is everything going at school?"

Perhaps I had a particularly stressful day, or maybe my blood sugar was abnormally low and I needed to eat more dinner. I must have been repressing all of my frustrations, discouragements, and petty gripes because my dad's question lifted a floodgate that released all of my negative emotions at once. Even if I had been aware of the intensity of these feelings, I would have struggled to hold them back. Without realizing what was happening, my mind was suddenly filled with everything I had been wanting to tell someone but had no one to tell it to. There is no way my parents could have anticipated the wave of emotions this simple question would release. They were just being parents, trying to stay connected to their young adult son who just graduated college and moved even farther from home. This wasn't a therapy session, just a short phone conversation on a Tuesday night. I have never been the type to cry out of frustration. There are plenty of events that trigger crying for me, such as a movie with a sad, or happy, ending, a public exhibition of someone doing something really awesome, or even regret. But, my emotional release mechanism of choice for frustration, discouragement, or disappointment is to rant, and it can be quite epic. Whether it was about my lack of playing time on various sports teams, not getting cast in the role I was hoping for in a theatre production, or any other circumstances in life not going my way, ranting was always my way of blowing off steam.

So, when my dad asked me how my teaching was going, it was not the first time he had been the audience to one of my rants. I don't think that was what surprised him. I think it was the tone and subject matter of this particular rant that took him by surprise. Most of my rants originated from the belief that I deserved better than I got. I was the best singer in the audition and should have gotten the part. I am a good athlete and work hard, so I should be getting more playing time. My teacher graded my paper more harshly than anyone else's because she doesn't like me or expects more of me or doesn't understand my style.

In hindsight, my feelings in this moment were valid, but my delivery was over the top. I spoke in absolutes, using words like "always" and "never." I exaggerated details while failing to acknowledge many of the successes I was experiencing alongside my failures. I refused to reframe my failings as signs of growth or progress. My words flowed out as steady and swiftly as a mountain brook suddenly swollen by a relentless storm. On my side of the phone was a pacing lunatic in a one-bedroom apartment, only constrained by the length of the telephone chord. On the other end sat two parents staring at each other across the room as they listened in on two separate telephones. If I could go back and relive this conversation, I would ease up on the melodrama. I began to explain to my dad how I should have never been allowed to graduate from college. Had my professors known how much time I spent skiing and mountain biking and watching movies and going to parties and trying to impress coeds, they would have never given me a degree. Sure, I did all of my assignments and attended class. I put on all the *appearances* of a good student, but it was all an act. My heart and mind were not focused on what I was there to learn. Any other student in my program probably acquired all of the necessary knowledge, skills, and abilities to be a successful teacher. No behavior problems, no piles of ungraded papers, no incoherent lessons, no disorganized grade book. Why? Because they paid attention. They were genuinely interested in learning how to teach. I was just going through the motions, and any success I had in my field placements was dumb luck. I was a mistake, the result of an imperfect system incapable of catching every false positive in their program. The fruit of all my effort in my teacher preparation program was a failed attempt at real teaching.

I had slipped through the cracks.

My mom and dad sat silently on the other end of the telephone line through this entire rant. They didn't try to stop and correct me. There were no attempts at setting the record straight or reminding me about recognitions I had received or encouraging words from my professors. They didn't mention how much of a positive impression I made at the job fair and subsequent interviews when I got my job. Based on their own experiences, they knew how hard it was learning a new career and I was growing more than I was failing, even if it didn't feel like it at the moment. They just listened and let me verbalize every single thought that was on my mind, every doubt I had harbored in my soul. And when I was finally done, they told me they loved me and encouraged me to take a shower and go to bed. They wanted me to believe a good night's rest would help me clear my head and shed some of the frustrations I was feeling. I knew I had exhausted and worried and maybe even scared them, and it was time to end the call. We said our goodbyes, and the click of the receiver of the phone hitting its base was the last sound followed by a long, eerie silence. I just stared at the wall, replaying highlights of the rant I had vomited on my parents.

Eventually, I got up and headed toward my bedroom when the phone rang. It was my dad. There was something he wanted to remind me of.

"Curby, you can always quit this job and come home. If this is as bad as you say, you aren't stuck there. No one is making you stay, and maybe you shouldn't."

"Thanks, Dad. No, I will tough it out until the end of the year and decide what to do next."

This was all I needed to hear at that moment. I was not going to show up to work the next day and be noticeably better at my job. My shortcomings as a teacher would not magically go away or be resolved by the end of the week. When I woke up the next morning, I may still be a rookie, but I was not a quitter.

I had never quit anything in my entire life. Not a musical production, not a class, not a sports team. Nothing. This teaching job was no different. Quitting means giving up on yourself, giving up on the people who are relying on you, and giving up on your belief in the ability to withstand uncomfortable, or even painful, circumstances. I was not in danger. I was not at risk for hurting myself or someone else (unless you consider not properly learning long division a form of harm). I was not passing a point of no return, the consequences of which would be felt for years into the future. The only thing wrong in this situation was that I was new at something really hard to do and I was having a tougher time than I thought I would. The problem was not my students, my school, or my lack of training. The heart of the problem was that I had to be okay with being bad at something new, and it was causing an extreme case of reality shock like I had never been forced to confront at any other point in my life. I was experiencing what every person feels to some degree when they're doing something new: growing pains.

That conversation with my parents was a turning point for me as a teacher. For many people, including myself, the harshest words we ever hear come from ourselves. We hurl insults then put them on automatic replay. We expect more from ourselves than we would reasonably expect from another person. We forgive others and extend grace, yet we tend to imprison ourselves in regret and shame for years with no possibility for parole. Although it was not pleasant at the time, the only way to liberate myself was to release those negative thoughts into the open. The best gift my parents could have given me was to listen. I corralled all of the negative thoughts about myself that were living in the dark corners of my mind and exposed them to the daylight. Transforming those toxic ruminations into spoken words allowed me to see them from a new perspective. I would have never spoken to another person the way I was speaking to myself. Hearing those words out loud and seeing their impact on my parents helped me start to understand how they might be affecting me each moment of every day. My dad was right. Either quit this job and move on to something else, or see this new experience for what it was and learn from it.

When I showed up to the school the next day, I still had a lot of cracks. I knew those cracks would not repair themselves, and if I quit now I might live with them the rest of my life. I could also choose to let those cracks tell a story, recast them as a road map leading me toward the teacher I knew I would one day become.

CHAPTER 7 *Spaghetti*

MY SISTER AND I BEGAN WATCHING A SHOW on MTV when I was in college called *The Real World*, and the tagline of the show was, "This is the true story of seven strangers picked to live in a house and have their lives taped to find out what happens when people stop being polite and start getting real." The show exposed everything from the mundane, such as roommates talking about their favorite movies over cereal, to heated conflicts on race, religion, sexuality, and politics. We were riveted by this concept, and it became a frequent topic of conversation while I was home that summer. Of course, I was also living my own version of this show in a parallel world as I tried to adjust to life with roommates, most of whom I had no choice in selecting. Living with people who had different values, beliefs, and personal habits was all at once exciting, awkward, and eye-opening. It was also quite stressful. As a person who has always tried to maintain a polite, friendly public identity, I spent a lot of energy trying to keep the "real" parts of me hidden from my roommates. Given enough time, the less-desirable truths about ourselves we try to keep secret from others will eventually surface. Sometimes it happens unexpectedly. Sometimes you don't have a choice, like the first time I farted in front of my class.

When I was in second grade, I had the uncontrollable urge to pass gas during read-aloud time, which was an activity the teacher always did right after lunch. My family had just moved to Wyoming from Arkansas, and I was the new kid in the class. It was hard enough not knowing anyone and dealing with the strange tension a new kid feels between everyone trying to be helpful and friendly but also being viewed as an outsider in the friend groups formed the previous year. The tenuous bridge I had formed between myself and a handful of friends would most likely not be able to withstand the trauma of being known as the kid who ripped loud farts when the entire class was silently enraptured by a story about a pig and a spider becoming friends. This was the type of attention I actually worked quite hard to avoid. Children tend to avoid the stinky kid. Who could have predicted read-aloud time would become the battleground between classroom decorum and the natural functioning of a child's digestive system? But there I sat, seven years old, having to make a life and death choice between instant relief and my reputation in the second grade. As the pressure continued to build in my abdomen, I tried to slowly ease one out and hope to stay undetected. I knew enough about science to know it would be harder to trace the source of a smell than that of a sound. I committed, stepped over the point of no return, and a steady rumble, between two and three seconds, escaped from between my Toughskins and the tile floor. Immediately, I was trapped in a cage of glares from every angle in the classroom with nowhere to run, nowhere to hide. Every person in my class began laughing, including the teacher. Some of them held their noses and feigned passing out from the noxious smell, which was not nearly as bad as my classmates were pretending. In that moment, I pledged I would never let that happen to me again, and if it did, I would deny it to my grave. Thankfully, my second-grade classmates were much more forgiving than I may have given them credit for, and the rest of the day, month, and year rolled along without incident.

Years later, college degree in hand and new career well underway, I was dealing with much more challenging issues than testing the boundaries of socially acceptable behavior. Among the multitude of adult realities I was now forced to deal with, perhaps the toughest new adulting habit to establish was how to stay fed and nourished. College life, which should have been the ideal training ground for learning how to plan, buy, ration, and prepare healthy meal options for myself instead devolved into a circuit of fast food, all-you-can-eat buffets, and various cafes on campus. Pretty much anything counted as a meal: a bag of Oreos or Doritos, a bagel with cream cheese, apple slices with peanut butter, or two pieces of cake. After about a week of teaching, I realized that the eating habits from my past were no longer sustainable, and one of the byproducts of my checkered culinary rap sheet was my inability to make a decent lunch for myself.

Even during my student teaching semester, which should have been an ideal opportunity to learn some of the less educative aspects of the teacher lifestyle, went down as yet another blown opportunity. The cafeteria at the school where I was teaching sold lunches for about two dollars, and I found it much easier to eat the school lunches than to go through the trouble of buying groceries and making lunch. Adulthood was deferred for at least another semester. Of course, these lunches were not your typical school lunch. The school where I was student teaching was nestled in a valley at the base of some mountains in Utah, and the meals in this school of about four hundred students were home cooked with love each day. Other than my one-year stint waiting tables, which came with one free meal per shift, this was probably the best food I had eaten on a consistent basis during my four years of college.

Of course, food preparation was only one of many reality shocks I was dealing with. I was also confronted with endless piles of papers to grade, lessons to plan, and a classroom full of children whose cooperation I tried to gain in long enough stretches to get through a full lesson. After about two weeks, the workload became almost too much to bear. I found myself staying at school until nine o'clock each night to catch up on work, only to get knocked over by another tidal wave of papers and planning the next day. By the time I made the twenty-minute commute home every night, I barely had enough energy to fix dinner, make my lunch for the next day, brush my teeth, and collapse into bed. So it should come as no surprise that two weeks into my first year of teaching I crashed into bed and forgot to make my lunch for the next day.

Looking back, the problem originated with my alarm clock and a simple user error. I accidentally turned my alarm off that morning instead of hitting the snooze button, giving me forty minutes of extra sleep.

I jerked out of bed, heart racing, overcome with panic and staring into the immediate reality of having only twenty minutes to shower and dress, gather my things, and get into my car. I reached into the refrigerator to get the lunch I never made. With no time to build my lunch, I groaned as I thought about having to stand in line with the kids during my "off" time, not to mention being forced to choose between green Jell-O and canned fruit salad with peeled grapes that looked like eyeballs. Out of time and ideas, I convinced myself that eating a school lunch just this once wouldn't be so bad.

The rest of the morning proceeded just as it had begun. It was Friday, and I had an enormous amount of information to cover that day. As usual, I was behind on several of my lessons, and I didn't want to put anything off until Monday. The next week posed its own adventures, and a fresh start to the week seemed appealing. So, I helped the students get settled, and we trudged through a variety of lessons until lunch. As we lined up for our walk to the cafeteria, a student called out from somewhere in the line.

"Mr. Alexander, we never took the spelling test!"

The weekly spelling test. A stalwart elementary school tradition older perhaps than language itself. When it came to generating grades to put in the gradebook, spelling tests were more dependable than Maytag, and more predictable than death and taxes. They were one of the few academic exercises to provide insight into weekly learning gains between the pre- and post-test. That unifying element of the schooling experience that distinguishes the US orthographically from the Canadians and British. In my haste to get caught up on some other lessons, I absentmindedly breezed past the one element of the language arts curriculum one would assume is the easiest to remember.

"We'll do it after lunch." With that, we filed out of the classroom.

Just a couple of minutes in the lunch line was all I needed to remind me I was no longer in Utah waiting on a lunch in that quaint school nestled between the Bear River Mountains and pristine farmland. The cooks on the other side of the glass seemed friendly, and I know they took pride in what they prepared. It just seemed so . . . parsimonious. The food was served on Styrofoam trays in relatively small portions, and the glossy, illustrated menu taped to the wall suggested it was printed for every child in the district. From my own elementary school in Wyoming where kids walked home at lunch and were welcomed with warm soup and grilled cheese to the industrial efficiency of suburban Texas, lunch suddenly seemed like a metaphor for my life spanning from childhood to the present.

I peeked over my students' heads to get a preview of the day's main entrée: spaghetti with meat sauce and garlic bread, which was really half of a hotdog bun smothered with salt and margarine. It was Friday, I was exhausted and hungry, and I didn't have the energy to be a food critic. I carried my tray into the teacher's lounge, slumped into a chair next to the other teachers, and picked through the noodles, trying to avoid the large pools of grease lurking at the bottom of the tray. I finished just in time to pick up my class from the playground and conclude my second full week of teaching.

The door to the playground was where I felt the first grumble in my stomach. Was it the grease? Too much garlic butter on the hot dog bun? Who knows? This was no time for pathology. I knew this feeling, and past experience taught me this was not going to go away silently. I think most people eventually learn to read the signs their bodies send them: aches in the knee from an old football injury prelude a change in the weather, headaches in certain parts of the cranium signify too much, or too little, caffeine, blemishes tell us not to eat so much greasy food. I knew my signs well, and one of them just appeared. My nemesis was lurking, watching, hiding in the shadows. He knew I was aware of his presence. He knew I was looking for any piece of evidence to convince myself he wasn't there.

After a quick round of drinks from the water fountain and a trip to the restroom, my class settled into their seats for read-aloud time. I would usually read a chapter from a book to help my students settle down and focus after recess. This time in the day had become sacred, allowing us to collectively feast on a rich banquet of words, characters, adventures, and unexpected plot twists. Over the years, I developed a list of essential read-alouds for my class, and I would anticipate each one like a child waiting for Christmas, knowing the beauty and wonder waiting for us, eager to see how each of my favorite books would grow in the fresh, fertile minds of each unique blend of students.

Somewhere about halfway through a chapter of *Matilda*, the nemesis rose up again, this time with slightly more force and sense of foreboding.

The book chapter flew by, and I asked the children to get out a piece of paper and their pencils so we could take the spelling test. The sound of shuffling papers and hushed chatter ebbed slightly, and within a couple of minutes the class was ready to proceed. So was the unwelcome visitor. Perhaps it was my standing and walking around the room. Maybe it was punishment for forgetting to make a better lunch, or for sloppy teaching earlier in the day. The reason does not matter. The spelling test became the point of assault, and my bowels were the battleground.

Mia was sitting in the front row of the class, right in the middle. Her placement alone should tell you something about Mia. In college, where students can pick their own seats, the front two rows and seats toward the center of the room are considered optimal for learning. My college-instructor parents told me this before I started college, so I dutifully sat in the front row in just about every class for four years. In elementary school, where seats are assigned, being placed in the front row has an entirely different meaning. In many cases, a student's placement toward the front of the classroom corresponds with the teacher's need to keep an eye on that student. Calling her easily distracted would be an insult to understatements. When Mia wasn't turned around in her seat talking to anyone who would listen, she was out of her seat getting a drink, sharpening her pencil, blowing her nose. Mia reminded me of Ramona Quimby, imaginative, quirky, and meddlesome. If Mia was not the child coming straight to me after recess to report whatever drama happened to unfold between her and her squad of friends, she was standing right next to the person doing the reporting, arms folded, nodding in agreement, adding details when necessary. But the characteristic that most defined Mia was her instinctive impulse to say whatever was on her mind.

We were at "near" on the spelling test when the first attack hit me. Luckily, I was near the door, and I managed to aim it into the hall. I used my clipboard to fan away any fumes that might follow me back into the classroom. I was sauntering back to the front of the room, so I could call out "deer" when the enemy countered with a surprise attack. I must have released the airlock while in stride, and a fog of indescribable atrocity instantaneously wreaked havoc on the first two rows of students. Sitting at ground zero was Mia, who was not known for her tact. As expected, she was not able to contain her reaction to the biological warfare that had just contaminated the clean air supply.

She stopped writing and dropped her pencil. It rolled off her uneven desk and bounced twice on the beige carpet. She began to writhe in pain, contorting her face into ghastly expressions, all the while blurting out exclamations like, "Oh my God!" and "Oh, jeez!" while wheezing and coughing loudly and uncontrollably. Even for the students in her vicinity who surely knew what was going on, her performance seemed a bit melodramatic.

She escalated her display by pulling her shirt over her face, holding it under her eyes with one hand and attempting to write with the other while stabilizing the test paper with her bony elbow. The rest of the class just stared at her, unsure of how to respond. The nemesis hung in the air, having now seized one-third of the room, watching with satisfaction the havoc about to unfold before me.

I was wasting precious time while Mia made no attempt to compose herself. Now was the time to take control, but I knew that even mentioning the crime would cause bedlam.

"Mia," I calmly asked, "are you okay?" I played dumb while trying to suppress the latent immature third grader deep inside me who wanted to laugh out loud.

"Okay? How can I possibly be okay? There is no way anyone in this room is okay right now. *No way!* Do you even know how to smell?"

"Mia, you really need to settle down. You are making a scene and disturbing your classmates who want to do well on the spelling test." I will never understand the supernatural grace that prevented me from bursting into laughter at that moment.

"Mr. A., you are seriously worried about the *spelling test* right now? We have *way* bigger problems than these spelling words!"

"Problems? Like what, Mia? What problems are you talking about?"

Her face emerged from the now-stretched shirt, she quickly pivoted, pointed her skinny finger and shouted, "Scotty!"

The nemesis had done his work as unrestrained chaos rippled across the classroom like a meteor landing in the ocean. The entire class all pulled *their* shirts up, pointed their fingers and commenced in a ritual of social banishment. Scotty pleaded his case in vain, explaining that he smelled it, too. He tried to pull his shirt up in solidarity with the rest of the class, but it was too late. I stared at the scene, conflicted, knowing on one hand, Scotty might never regain his dignity, but justifying my silence with the belief that children are much more resilient than my reputation. Had I admitted I was the source of the nemesis, this would become my defining story, the first thing students thought of when they heard my name. Among this group of kids, at least six of them had younger siblings. Even if they weren't in my class, they would be in fourth grade within the next four years. This story would be passed down like Grandma's hand-painted vase for years to come. It may have outlived me. The class was in complete disorder, and Scotty was pleading for his classmates to let him back onto the Ark, but my credibility had been preserved.

Thankfully, children move on pretty quickly. This episode faded by the time the class was leaving for music, and there was a general consensus Scotty was not responsible for the horror unleashed on the class just a couple of hours earlier. I had a talk with Mia about how it is not polite to blame people for something they may not have done. I stressed the importance of keeping certain thoughts to herself, even if she had a strong urge to let it out. She retorted that some people should keep certain things to themselves even when they have the urge to let it out. I will never know to whom that comment was directed.

When I consider everything going on in my life at the time, this event was insignificant. This was my first year as a teacher, and every day was hard. I had to choose to see the positive in the tiniest victories. I spent more nights lying awake than in slumber. I could barely afford to buy groceries, and I got lost every time I tried to go somewhere. All my friends were more than a thousand miles away. Yet, in those times when I was able to visit my relatives a couple of hours away or chat with coworkers, in midst of this struggle, I was still able to laugh. Sometimes

I would retell this very story, knowing it would get a laugh or two. We can always extrapolate humor from our misery, find some comedy in the struggle, and ease the burden from our soul for a moment. Not everything I experienced was funny or appropriate to joke about, but laughter saved me that year. Instead of constantly lamenting about my hardships, I revisited the events of each day, searching for the take-away lesson or story, filtering it with my own brand of humor.

A few months later, I found myself in the same predicament. Busy morning, no lunch, a decision to make. I opened the fridge and scanned the contents as a cool vapor washed over me. My options were limited, and I needed to make a decision. I grabbed the package of lunch meat, some cheese, and the half loaf of bread sitting there. Today I would make my sandwich on the fly. Toss in a cup of yogurt and a bag of chips for good measure, and I was on my way a little wiser, perhaps slightly more confident to find my way through the maze of adulting.

As I bounced down the steps toward my truck, I rehearsed what I would tell the students once they were in their seats: "Get out your pencils and paper, class. We're taking the spelling test first today."

# CHAPTER 8 *The Comparison Trap*

EACH NIGHT AS I FELL ASLEEP, I would pray for renewed energy to make the new day better than the last. Whether it was handling classroom disruptions with a little more patience, or explaining a concept a little more clearly, or leaving my desk a little more organized than it was the day before, I was determined to learn from this endless list of teachable experiences. Most days I would see glimpses of progress, but sometimes I would go back to sleep feeling like I was stuck in an endless cycle of trying and failing, making plans and watching them fall apart. Perhaps my expectations were unrealistic, blinding me from the small improvements and victories that happened on even the worst days.

By this time in the year, I had started to make some new friends. A friend from college moved to another suburb a little over an hour away, and we would get together now and then. I went to a baseball game with some other teachers at my school, and they also invited me to a downtown art festival. My social calendar was not full by anyone's standards, but at least I wasn't sitting at home all the time by myself. I was still working through my struggles at work, which caused a different kind of nagging loneliness I didn't know how to deal with.

For the first time in my life, I felt alone in my struggle. No matter how much positive self-talk I used to prop myself back up when I stumbled, I carried the weight of feeling as if I were the only person experiencing—perhaps the only person to have ever experienced—this chronic sense of inadequacy. The worst kind of loneliness, I learned, was not caused by a lack of company. It was the belief that no one understood what I was going through.

There were four other first-year teachers who started at the same time as me in my building. For the first three months of the school year, I barely interacted with any of them. I would pass them in the halls, see them in the teachers' lunchroom, and sit across the room from them at faculty meetings, but we never really had any sort of conversation. Most of the new teachers were in a much different set of circumstances than I was. Two of them were recently married, one of them grew up in the suburb where we were teaching and lived at home, and the one whom I knew the best lived on a totally different side of the city and was one of those extroverted types who made friends with anyone and already had a party squad to hang out with on the weekends. Her name was Rachel, and she taught fifth grade. She was the teacher in the building with whom I had the most in common. And by "in common," I mean we were both from out of state, we both recently graduated from college, and we were both trying to learn the nuances of a new career and city simultaneously.

I happened to sit next to Rachel at a faculty meeting about halfway through the school year, and I just had to know how the other new teachers were doing. I would occasionally wonder whether I was causing my students to regress in their academic progress. Had I unintentionally undone the hard work of all the teachers my students had in the past? In my heart, I knew the students were making progress, but I couldn't help but compare myself to the other teachers, like Rachel. The only other first-year teacher about whom I had any intel was Sarah, and even though I know the assistant principal had good intentions, the vivid descriptions she gave me about Sarah's intrinsic knack for teaching left me feeling worse than before the conversation started. Not only did she go into specific details about the pedagogical, classroom management, and motivation strategies that made her amazing—none of which described my own classroom practice—but she also made it clear that Sarah had the "it" factor when it came to teaching.

"She's got it. Sarah is an amazing teacher. She knew exactly what every kid in her class was doing. It was so much fun to watch. Wow! She just has what it takes!"

Did this mean she believed I could also have what it takes, given enough time and effort? Or was she telling me "either you have it or you don't," and this was her subtle way of breaking it to me. "And you, young man, are no Sarah!" If I looked closely, I could see the comparison gremlin showing its ugly face, taunting and teasing me from the back of the classroom.

So here I was, sitting next to Rachel in a faculty meeting, desperate to know if I was the only teacher in the building struggling so hard. I wanted to know if I was as alone as I felt most of the time.

"Hey, Rachel, how is everything going?"

"Oh, things are great. I am so busy! I don't think I have been so tired in my entire life." Well, we had that in common. I was exhausted all the time, but it seemed to get more intense as the week progressed. This conversation took place on a Thursday, which meant I was already running on fumes.

"Yeah, I know. I am so tired all the time, but at least we have the weekend to catch up on sleep." This was a total lie. I have never been the type to sleep all weekend, and I already knew I was bringing a gigantic stack of work home with me. "So," I continued. "How is your teaching going? I mean, besides being tired and busy with so much to do. Do you ever struggle?" This was my attempt at steering the conversation toward myself and my own struggles.

"Well, you know, I have some days where I feel more prepared than others, but overall things are going pretty well. I have a sweet group of kids, and they are so smart! Oh my gosh, their writing is just amazing, and the parents have been so supportive all year. We are just having a blast!"

This was not what I wanted to hear. I could barely get five sentences out of most of my students, even from those who I knew probably wrote a lot the previous year. I mean, these kids were in fourth grade, for heaven's sake! I was not expecting them to be little adults or write like Hemingway, but I didn't think I was unreasonable to expect more than two sentences.

Out of the twenty-one students in my class, there were about three who routinely gave their best effort, perhaps two more who gave enough effort to get by, even though I knew it wasn't their best, and the remaining sixteen students in my class were floating somewhere between being completely lost and enjoying the bliss of having a clueless rookie for a teacher.

Their parents were mostly supportive, even though I had some bad encounters with a couple of them. Those negative encounters had definitely put me on notice, planted the seed that I, not their children, was the source of the problems in my classroom. Rachel's last sentence, however, was the hardest to process. She and her students were having a blast? A blast? Are you kidding me? Rachel did not try to explain what she meant by this term. I imagined this intimate community of happy students and their happy teacher, smiling, laughing, exuberant over all the amazing skills and facts they were learning. Her classroom full of eager fifth graders, all hunched over their journals scratching out every little detail from their vivid imaginations, begging for more time when Rachel told them to wrap up their last sentence. I was surrounded by the sound of pencil lead rubbing against paper, like sandpaper smoothing rough edges into clarity or whispers from a muse breathing new ideas to life. The students sitting on the edge of their chairs, clutching their journals, eagerly waving their hands in the air in hopes of being chosen to read their latest masterpiece to the rest of the class. They laughed, they cried, they connected with each other at the deepest possible level, and at the end of the day they couldn't wait to come back to school and do it all over again. What a blast! I was at once jealous, resentful, and hopeful, thinking that one day I would describe my teaching, my classroom, my relationship with my students, as a blast.

"How about you? How are you doing?"

I decided not to delve into my own problems, mainly because the faculty meeting was about to start. As much as I wanted to just let it all come flooding out and talk to someone about my feelings of incompetence and lack of proper preparation, my frustration with the students in my class, my feelings of being alone and stranded like a castaway, I knew this was not the time or place to have that conversation. I also knew that if I spewed every single emotion I was feeling in that moment on Rachel, she might never want to talk to me again. As sad as it was, Rachel was the closest thing I had to a friend at work.

I chose to view this as confirmation about a truth I was certain needed no additional proof. I was the only teacher in the building, maybe even in the entire district, who felt lost, inadequate, and confused. How public this information was, I had no idea. My teaching partners, who ultimately helped me out of my hole, advocated for me, and became my greatest fans, definitely knew about my struggles. Had they told anyone else? Probably not directly, but I am sure other teachers in the building could see the evidence for themselves: The restless students in school assemblies, the loud, serpentine line of students walking behind me in the halls. Just the sheer amount of noise coming from my classroom in general was probably all the proof any seasoned teacher would need to come to the conclusion that I did not exactly have things under control. On a deep and personal level, these feelings of incompetence and ineffectiveness as a new teacher were the most extreme sense of loneliness I have ever experienced in my life. Being so bad at something new is frustrating; succumbing to the fallacy that no one else on the planet has experienced these emotions brings shame and humiliation. It is loneliness fueled by the fear of being exposed as a phony.

I let down my guard as the year went on, one small step at a time. I initiated conversations with the other first-year teachers at lunch or meetings, and we would swap stories about funny things the kids said or little mistakes we made throughout the day. The laughter was disarming and real and therapeutic. Since we were all teaching different grade levels, we were able to see similar issues from a different perspective. Sure, it's hard getting fourth graders to write an essay, but imagine trying to get kindergarteners to write a sentence! Sharing our experiences with each other gave me assurance that, even in the midst of my imperfect situation, I was not alone. Despite the confident appearances we were determined to project, we were all struggling in some way. I was struggling in one area, while Rachel felt inadequate about something completely different, and Sarah's dilemma was something I had never even considered. The more I realized we were all trudging our chosen path in one way or another, the less alone I felt in my journey.

There are countless songs, poems, books, quotes, and movies about how, no matter the way things seem, you are not alone. This theme repeats itself so often because it's true. I was living in a quiet apartment, and I barely knew anyone in the town where I was living, but I was not alone. At times I felt like a failure, as if I had somehow slipped past security in the teacher preparation process, an imposter in a profession where everyone else seemed to be an expert. What I began to realize as the year progressed was that everyone, no matter how well put together they seem on the outside, is dealing with something. We all have fears and insecurities, areas in need of improvement, tasks and responsibilities (and people) that may need more attention than we are giving them. My struggle did not mean I was alone. In fact, I began to see it as my strongest source of connection.

# CHAPTER 9 *Arrows*

I REMEMBER READING SOMETHING IN THE BIBLE one time about children being like arrows in the hand of a warrior. I'm pretty sure this verse applied to parents and their children, but my mind would come back to this passage quite a bit as a teacher. I guess I really had no right to refer to this verse because, as hard as teaching was at times, I was only with them for a fixed amount of time before they went home and eventually moved to the next grade. Seven and a half hours per day, five days per week, for thirty-six weeks. As much responsibility as I felt for taking part in their success, there was only so much I could do in 180 days. Even the most difficult child went home at the end of the day while I got to recuperate in the quiet confines of my apartment. For the parents of my students, this was a lifetime commitment. Maybe I was being presumptuous when I appropriated this verse to describe my responsibility to my students, but it still resonated with me.

Like many Bible verses, the meaning was lost on me during my youth. Perhaps it is by design that in our youth, when so many of us have no choice but to attend church with our families, so much of the Bible doesn't make much sense at all and we watch the minute hand on the clock until we can go home. At least for me, once I was out on my own making my own decisions, many of those verses began to make sense.

That was certainly true of the verse about arrows and children.

I was not an expert archer, but I had spent some time shooting at targets either in my backyard, at our cabin on the mountain, or, of all places, in PE at school. I can still hear my PE teacher walking us through the steps of proper shooting technique. He emphasized to the class how important it was to have your feet set properly because we wanted our bodies to be as stable as possible. I remember looking down at my feet to make sure they were set slightly wider than shoulder width apart. Had my feet been too close together, I would be unstable. If they were too wide, I could lose some mobility. When it came to shooting an arrow, I needed to have a solid foundation. I positioned my body perpendicular to the target in order to draw the bow across my chest.

The next step involved placement of the arrow on the bow. The teacher instructed us to place the front of the arrow on the rest above the grip in our left hand. The back of the arrow had three feathers, one index and two fletchings, and we were told to position the bowstring in the nock so the index feather was facing away from the bow. If we didn't set the arrow correctly, the index feather might scrape against the bow, get ripped from the shaft, and permanently affect the arrow's ability to fly straight. So, even in archery, everything had its place.

Once our feet and the arrow were in their proper position, the teacher told us to hold the bow in our left hand with our left arm straight out directly in front of us. He modeled how to pull the bowstring and arrow back until our hand rested directly below our right ear. We were instructed to look down the shaft of the arrow and aim the point at the bullseye. On his command, we could release the bowstring and let the arrow fly toward the center of the target.

After waiting patiently for my turn, I remember stepping up to the line with the bow in my left hand. Having gotten a bow and arrow set for Christmas the year before—nearly identical to the one I was holding—I was convinced this would be my Red Ryder BB gun moment. While everyone else in my class was figuring out the basics of this ancient apparatus, I had unlocked the aeronautical mysteries of the archer's science within the fenced-in training ground of my backyard. As the class panned back and forth across the debris field scattered with misguided darts, a single beam of light would illuminate my solitary hay-packed target with all three arrows clustered in the bullseye.

I set my feet into a square stance, digging my right foot into the dirt for extra stability. Breathe. On the teacher's command, I nocked my first arrow and relaxed my shoulders, allowing the bow to hang at my side.

"Okay, class, draw your bows." Breathe. I stared down the target, blocking out everything but the small yellow dot in the middle.

"Hold it until I tell you to shoot." I envisioned the burning and twitching in the shoulders of my classmates from the anaerobic demand placed on their deltoids as I stood steadfast, galvanized by the six or seven times I had used my own bow and arrow over the last few months. Breathe.

"Shoot!" I waited for the others in my class to hurl their bolt toward its destination, hoping that being the last to shoot would focus the attention of the class on what was about to happen. About half the class hit the target but lacked the momentum for it to stick, so the arrows bounced off the target and fell to the ground. Two students were able to get their arrows to stick in the target, but from where I was standing, I couldn't see how close they were to the bullseye.

I took one last breath, then slowly exhaled the last of the air from my lungs. Staring directly at the bullseye, I released the fingers on my right hand and felt the bowstring snap from my grip.

I stood in silence as I watched the arrow sail over the top of the target and skip along the blacktop on the playground.

Notoriety, it seemed, would have to be found in other pursuits.

That experience evoked memories of the final scene from *Robin and Marian,* a movie I remember watching on TV with my mom. Robin, with his most loyal companion, Little John, returned to England from many hard years fighting alongside Richard the Lionhearted in the Crusades and in France to rekindle his unrequited love for Maid Marian, who was serving as an abbess for the Roman Catholic Church. Robin quickly reunited with Will Scarlett and Friar Tuck, only to learn Prince John had become king and continued to terrorize the people of England with his main henchman, the Sheriff of Nottingham. After a series of heroic rebellions, Robin was mortally wounded and lay dying in Marian's abbey. In his final act, he begged Little John for one last request, best captured in the words of Eugene Field:

> *"Give me my bow,"* said Robin Hood,
> *"An arrow give to me;*
> *And where't is shot mark thou that spot,*
> *For there my grave shall be."*

Sean Connery as Robin Hood released the fateful arrow with what remained of his strength, and the closing scene of the movie showed the arrow soaring out the window of the abbey toward his final sanctuary, Sherwood Forest. The viewer never saw where the arrow landed.

Here I stood, an unskilled archer standing in front of my quiver full of arrows—actually someone else's arrows but whose fourth-grade education had been entrusted to me. I spent the best hours of the day showing them everything's place—commas and periods, numbers and letters, people, and features on a map—and making sure they made it to the right place at the right time all day long. If they did everything right, if they never stepped out of line and made sure they knew where everything was supposed to go, where did that leave them?

I showed up every day to teach, but I questioned whether or not anything I did was inspiring. Was I playing it safe just teaching the basics, or had I pulled back the bow with all my strength and helped launch them into an unknown future? I had no understanding, no control, over where any of them would land. I would probably never know how most of these kids would turn out, how much education they would pursue, what they chose to do with their lives, and the only thing I seemed to have any control over was cultivating the skills, attitudes, and behaviors that would help them along the way, no matter where they decided to go.

Teaching was hard enough without trying to predict which of my students would develop a cure for the next pandemic or invent the one kitchen appliance no household could live without. I barely knew what I was going to teach from week to week, so I had no predictions about whether or not I was aiming at the right things.

Was my main priority to make sure my students just learned the next lesson, in hopes they would be able to string enough of them together to swing into the next grade?

Maybe my job was to help them understand the big questions we have all wrestled with—who am I, why do I exist, and what is my place in the universe. These are the same questions people have been asking for thousands of years. Trying to find the answers is missing the point. The purpose of the journey is discovering, despite our many differences, our hearts beat the same way.

I guess I could let the students discover their own interests through projects or whatever they wanted to do. They may not learn to read or do math, but they sure would have a lot of fun along the way.

Becoming educated, it seemed, was more than figuring out where everything goes. It's also about deciding where you want to go and finding your place in the world.

# CHAPTER 10 *Conferences with Parents*

COLBY WAS A TRANSFER STUDENT IN MY CLASS. He had recently moved to town from a different area of the city, and he was having difficulty adjusting to the culture of his new school. Every class has its own collective personality. Some classes you can tell jokes and be silly, but when it's time to get back to work they can quickly switch gears. Other classes hear a joke and think it's "open mic night," and whatever hope there was for staying on schedule suddenly vanishes. Some classes like to work to music, while others need a quiet room. Some classes get along and become great friends; some classes never experience sustained peace.

The class culture Colby joined was generally amicable with very few instances of squabbling or tattling on each other. As I was about to find out, this class was also predominantly comprised of Goody Two-shoes. Don't get me wrong. I will take a classroom full of rule-followers any day over a bunch of liars, sneaks, or cheaters. This classroom dynamic just so happened to not work in Colby's favor because . . . well, he had a potty mouth, and he just so happened to be surrounded by kids who placed cussing right up there with murder, robbing banks, and starting nuclear war.

Every primary teacher throughout history knows that feeling of being gang rushed at the end of recess by a jury of do-gooders. They witnessed something, or claim to know someone else who did, and they can't wait to tell the teacher. You've seen their up-tempo march in unison, calling out your name before they arrive, all talking at once to tell you what just went down. You've seen the aggrieved "and what are you going to do about it" expression on each face as you try to calm everyone down, at least enough to be able to teach math. From the moment Colby arrived in my classroom, this happened almost every day.

"Mr. Alexander, we just heard Colby use the F-word!"

"Did you actually hear it yourself, or did someone tell you they heard it?"

"Jenene says she actually heard it!"

"Jenene, is that true? Did you hear Colby use a bad word?"

"I think so."

"Thank you for telling me. I'll talk to Colby about it."

Tattling is a strange thing. It almost always involves something a child knows they shouldn't be doing, but it's used in a way just to get another kid in trouble. Justice used as a weapon. Were these girls really that offended by the F-word? Maybe, but there was an unmistakable hint of glee in their voices as they knew they had the evidence needed to put the new kid in his place.

I talked to Colby, and there was just enough emotion in his denial of the accusation that I knew beyond reasonable doubt he had in fact dropped the F-bomb at recess. I gave a general reminder about language and appropriateness and the difference between what we hear in movies (or at home!) and how we talk in public. He glared at the lead juror as he walked back to his seat while she smirked back at him.

This event repeated itself every single day, and it was not always the same children tattling on Colby. After a week or so of colorful recess discourse, multiple conversations with Colby, and even a spontaneous classroom meeting, I knew it was time to address this head on. Colby's bad language, combined with his tendency to not complete assignments, was enough justification to schedule a meeting with his mom.

We corresponded through notes back and forth, with Colby as the messenger, for a few days and finally settled on a time. Colby's mom worked the early morning shift at her job, which was on the other side of Dallas. She typically left for work at 6 a.m., which was the only time she was able to come to the school and meet with me. Colby was probably waking up each morning to an empty house, and it was up to him and his brother to get themselves off to school. We scheduled a day to meet, which meant I had to make arrangements with our head custodian to access the building at six in the morning.

On the day of the meeting, I arrived a few minutes early to get my room ready for the conference. A small table sat in the back of the room near my desk, which is where most of my meetings with parents took place. The building was more than quiet. José and I were the only people there, and it felt still, cold, lifeless. Even the smallest, faintest of sounds echoed through the hallway. As I sat at the table reviewing the documents for the meeting—some samples of Colby's work and a copy of his progress report—I heard the mother and son coming up the hallway. They were talking, but I couldn't make out what they were saying. When they got close to the classroom, I looked up expecting to see them walk through the doorway, but their voices stopped by the door. I was shaken by a harsh flow of words rushing from who I assume was Colby's mom. In a raspy whisper, I couldn't understand what she was saying but it was clear she was angry with him. This made my heart ache for Colby. I couldn't discern whether she had cursed, but her tone communicated the true meaning of her message. I wondered if his mom saw this meeting, and even Colby, as an inconvenience. A few seconds later, they emerged into my room.

After some introductions and small talk, we started the meeting. I knew she had to head to work soon, so I tried to keep it brief. I started with some positive comments about Colby then moved on to discuss his missing work. His mom shared the difficulty she faced with keeping him on track in school because of the long hours she worked as a single parent and the long commute to and from her workplace. We discussed some strategies for how I could help Colby while he is at school, as well as some ideas for him prioritizing homework once school is over. We all seemed to agree this was a reasonable plan and we could all work together to stick to it.

The next item on my agenda was Colby's behavior: the cussing, lying, and fighting. My mind snapped back to that short interchange before they entered the room and the raw ugliness in her tone. I mentally lined up what I had planned to share next to what I knew I needed to say.

"Other than the homework issue, I am really glad to have Colby in my class. He has a lot of potential, and he is starting to make some friends." I looked directly at Colby as I spoke, "Colby, just like all kids his age, is learning how to behave, how to speak to others, and which words are appropriate or not. He has some work to do, but I'm proud of him for learning from his mistakes."

"Well, Mr. Alexander, I can promise you we don't tolerate bad language or disrespect at home, so if there is anything I can do to help, just let me know."

Colby's expression as he peeked at me sheepishly from the top of his eyes told me everything. He knew that I knew. He knew I heard his mom speak harshly to him outside my classroom door. He may have even known I knew she was not in a frame of mind to be receptive to negative news about her child. He also knew, in that moment, I was in his corner and that laying bare every peccadillo since he arrived would only make things worse. His mom was mad about having to come to the school at 6 a.m., about having to work so many hours so far from home, about having a child who added to her stress, and I was not going to fan the flames of her anger. "Colby's a good kid. You've got this, don't you, pal?"

"Yes, sir."

We made some more small talk as we walked toward the door, and I watched until Colby and his mom turned the corner into the main hallway. The reports of his fourth-grade code infractions on the playground seemed to happen less and less until I stopped hearing about his behavior at all. He still had some issues with completing work, but we found a way to get it done. We weren't always on the same page, but we were allies.

About three months later, I noticed Colby was not at school one day. Despite his behavior and academic issues, he had good attendance. Around midmorning, the secretary showed up at my door. "Colby needs to get his belongings. They are moving, and today is his last day. He refused to come to get his own stuff because he's been crying. He kept telling his mom how much he likes your class and doesn't want to move."

"Sandy, could you watch my class for a minute while I go talk to him?"

"No problem, Curby." I quickly stuffed the contents of his desk into a spare plastic bag and walked into the school office to find Colby sitting in defiance in one of the chairs, arms crossed, looking down.

"Hey, man. I hear you're leaving us. I don't know what those bossy girls are going to do without someone to keep tabs on." He had been trying so hard to stay mad, but he let a slight smile slip. "We're going to miss you, pal. You got off to a rough start, but I'm so glad you got to be part of my class. When you get to your new school, do your best to pick up where you left off."

"Yes, sir." I could see his lower lip starting to tremble as his eyes pooled with tears.

Some kids are dealt a bad hand. There are things they have to do without, they practically raise themselves as their parents are doing their best to provide, and nothing seems to come easy. Colby had been in my class three, maybe four months, tops. He was an outsider, a misfit, and if it was up to some of the kids in the class, he would have stayed that way. No one took the time to understand his story, and the kids just saw him as trouble. For a few minutes early one morning, I got a better view of what was really going on. Colby just wanted to be understood.

"Well, I need to get back to class. I just wanted to say goodbye and I hope you do great at your next school. I'm so proud of you, and I'm going to miss you." I stood up and turned toward the door.

"Thank you for all you did, Mr. Alexander." Colby's mom was standing off to the side holding the bag of school supplies. "I think this is the first time Colby has actually liked school. Things are rough for us right now, and we're moving in with my sister."

"Well, I hope you find a good school. Colby has what it takes to be successful, and I know he'll do great."

As I started walking, I felt Colby's arms reach around my waist. He didn't try to say anything, he just hugged me. I reached down and patted his back then tousled his hair. He eventually eased up, and I patted his shoulder one more time. He sniffed and wiped away tears. I walked toward the door, then turned back toward the office. Colby and I made eye contact, and I smiled and waved to him one last time. I took deep breaths as I walked back to the classroom, trying to loosen up the lump in my throat.

# CHAPTER 11 *Songs and Stories*

DURING MY JUNIOR YEAR OF COLLEGE, in a Language and Literacy class, I had to come up with a book activity to present to the rest of my classmates. The instructions were pretty clear: find a picture book, read it to the class, then create a follow-up activity based on the book. As soon as the professor finished explaining the assignment, the room exploded with ideas. Oh, how am I going to decide on just one book? Can I use two or three books from a collection? Can we use art supplies? My activity may require us to move the tables . . . is that okay? Everyone in the class, with the exception of one person, could not suppress their excitement for this project.

I was the exception. Other than the books my mom and dad read to me as a child, I could not think of one book title or author. Did the university library even have children's picture books to check out? I wasn't sure. I hid in silence as everyone else giddily danced through an exhaustive list of books, each one apparently better than the last.

My love affair with books officially started at a small bookstore in the local mall, where I had gone out of desperation to see if I could find a book for my class project. Even in this small bookstore chain nestled between a discount shoe store and some place selling trendy clothes, I was overwhelmed by the choices. The pictures, the stories, the subtle levels of humor aimed at both children and adults were captivating. My immediate dilemma was that I didn't have enough money to buy every single book in that section. I began creating a mental list of books to buy as the money became available.

I bought a couple of books that day, and one of them stood out immediately as the one I would use for my project. The root of my decision may have been a little narcissistic, but I wanted to base my project on *Alexander, Who Used to be Rich Last Sunday* by Judith Viorst. It told the story of a boy, Alexander, who was given a dollar by his grandparents when they came to visit on Sunday. The book chronicled each unlucky or unwise turn of events that caused the balance of his dollar to dwindle away, until he was left with nothing but a melted candle and a couple of bus tokens. I wondered if children living in rural Utah would get stumped by the concept of bus tokens. Other than that, it was a cute story with just the right amount of repetition, sentimental childhood humor, and a timeless moral.

The assignment was not complicated, but it required a lot of creativity, something I had never struggled with in the past. Where my content knowledge or understanding of children in general was lacking, I always had a creative way of crafting and presenting the requirements for my courses. One semester, I used fabric from the same pair of shorts for every single craft in my Preschool Methods course. My professor and classmates thought of me as their goofy little brother, compensating for my shortcomings with resourcefulness. These days we call it "grit," but I was just trying to complete my assignments without spending a lot of money.

I got home from the bookstore, plopped on my bed, and began reading through my new book again. I read each page slowly, scanning each of the pictures closely with the hope this would give me some inspiration, some sort of creative spark. The idea I had been hoping for came out of nowhere. As I read the lines of the book, I began crafting lyrics in my head. The story and the song soon became inseparable in my mind, and I reached for the guitar and began strumming chords.

I lumbered toward the front of the crowded college classroom holding only my book when it was my turn to present. Everyone in the class had already shared. I sat in a chair at the front of the room and read with as much expression as my one-year-as-a-theatre-major voice could summon. The book ended, and I looked up at the people sitting in the room. Some of them looked back, smiling, waiting for the second half of the project. Others looked away, avoiding eye contact, clearly embarrassed for me.

This was the last time my true identity was hidden to everyone. Clark Kent before the cape. Peter Parker before the web. I was the Singing Teacher, and no one even knew.

I stood and walked to the back of the room to retrieve my guitar case. The energy in the room suddenly spiked, and I could hear murmurs among my peers. Some people probably assumed I had not finished the assignment, or I had recklessly thrown something together at the last minute. The sound of the buzz rose as I walked toward the front of the room holding a guitar, then it ebbed once I sat back in the chair and rested the guitar on my leg. I handed one of my friends a stack of paper slips, each numbered on the back, along with a roll of tape. "Would you mind taping these up on the wall in this order? Just follow my lead."

My song was repetitive, repeating the chorus each time around and adding a new line at the end. Each new line represented one of the ways Alexander had wasted his money. Considering I had only learned these three chords a couple of weeks ago, I played with surprising confidence. Performing had never been a challenge. I played through the chords one time, then started in on the main chorus:

> *Both of my brothers are richer than me, but it wasn't always that way.*
> *I got a dollar from my grandma once upon a Sunday . . .*

Because of the repetition and simplicity of the lyrics, the class was singing along after the third time through without me even having to say, "Everybody now!"

My classmate faithfully put up each new line without once being prompted. I interacted with my captive audience to see if they could remember what line came next. In the course of those three minutes, we were laughing, singing, bobbing our heads, and smiling at each other. I had been preparing for this moment for two weeks, playing and singing, singing and playing, alone in my room for hours at a time. The tips of my fingers were calloused from fretting the chords over and over.

Before the last chord faded, the class erupted in applause. Questions were flying from every corner of the room, faster than I could answer. The professor asked in front of the class why I had never mentioned before how I could sing and play guitar. Talking about myself was something I generally avoided, and this was another reminder of how little I really knew my classmates. She encouraged me to contact the author of the book and sing her my song. Even while caught up in the hype of the moment, I knew it was not *that* good of a song. I looked out among the smiling faces as I put the guitar back in the case and removed the slips of paper from the wall.

My experience in the Language and Literacy class set the tone for the remainder of my time in college. Everywhere I went, every school where I was placed, included time spent singing silly songs I had written to go along with fun books we were reading. Some of the songs were instant classics, and others were performed once or twice then faded away due to lack of popularity.

One of my friends who had already graduated left his guitar in our house, and I used it for the next year and a half. I felt guilty taking someone else's instrument to Texas with me when I finished school, so I left it in the fraternity house and found myself without a guitar for the first time in four years. I may have mentioned this to my students, but I can't remember exactly how it came up or what I said.

All I know is that one day before the bell rang, Carter, a student in my class, showed up at my door with his dad with a smile as wide as his face and an old guitar case in his arms. His dad assured me it had been sitting in a closet for more years than Carter had been alive, and they were happy to see it get used again. I opened the case to discover an old brown guitar looking back at me. Our first introduction reminded me of those two-character movies: *Tommy Boy*, *Lethal Weapon*, *The Odd Couple*, *When Harry Met Sally*. They all start off with two characters, polar opposites, being placed together serendipitously and forming an unexpected partnership. By the end, you can't imagine one character without the other. Meeting this guitar felt a little like those movies.

The varnish had worn off in a few areas, and there were several knicks and scratches along the neck and body. The face of the guitar had a bird inlaid with mother of pearl, as well as a braid around the perimeter with the same material. It didn't take a hippie from the sixties to figure out this guitar had seen its fair share of hootenannies.

I lifted it from the case, set it on my knee, and strummed a G chord. The old bard strained at being summoned after such a long sabbatical, but I knew with a new set of strings this thing would play like Orpheus. I was grateful for the generosity and kind gesture from this family, knowing this guitar would be the source of many memories throughout the year. I thanked Carter and his dad repeatedly until I'm sure they felt sufficiently awkward, and I spent the remaining minutes preparing for the day ahead.

Carter stared at me expectantly all day. For the entire morning, he and I were the only two people in the room who knew what was hiding in my storage closet. Every time I used the word "next" or hinted we were about to start something new, his head would snap up and his eyes would beg, "Now? Please tell me you are going to get the guitar and play for us!" This pattern continued until lunch, when Carter pulled me aside as the class walked in single file to the cafeteria: "C'mon, Mr. A! Just one song! I brought the guitar all the way to school just for you!" I was trying to keep order as long as possible, and I had already made up my mind. "We'll see, Carter. We have so much to do this afternoon."

What Carter didn't know was I planned on teaching the class a couple of songs after lunch, no matter what. I have always preferred to surprise people rather than promise something with the possibility I may have to back out later. Once we were back in the classroom after lunch, the time I would have normally used to read from a chapter book, I walked to my storage closet and retrieved the guitar case. They began to buzz like Grand Central Station, whispering to each other and making song requests. Leave it to a fourth grader to ask, "Mr. Alexander, is that a guitar?" It would have been easy to make fun of the student's obvious question, but I opted for, "I'm not sure . . . let's check. Well, would you look at that? It *is* a guitar! What in the heck am I supposed to do with this thing?"

"Play it!"

"Play it? I've never seen one of these things in my life." I set the guitar back in the case and walked over to my desk. I picked up a dictionary and said to the class, "Here, give me a minute while I study how to play one of these . . . what did you call it, a guitar. It should only take a minute."

I quickly fanned the pages of the dictionary while moving my eyes quickly from side to side. I repeated this a couple of times, then set the book back on my desk. The children were watching me intently, not sure whether to laugh or stay quiet. Some of them, including Carter, had caught on to the prank and were smiling at each other. I walked back to the stool in the center of the room, picked up the guitar once again, and began to play. The same student who asked the original question blurted, "How did you learn to play so fast?" to which three or four different children shot back, "He already knew how! Jeez! He was just playing a trick on us!"

Over the next fifteen minutes, I taught them a song I wrote when I did part of my student teaching in a kindergarten class. It was called, "X Marks the Spot," and it involved me picking students to name the next place we were going to visit.

> *If I had an airplane, you and I could go,*
> *To the mountains way up high, or to the sea below!*

Just like the kindergarteners would do, every single kid in the class wanted their turn to say where we were going next. Some students named places dear to them, such as Oklahoma because that is where they visit Grandma, or Florida because they went there for vacation last summer. Other students tried to think of the most remote places on the planet, and a few even had the guts to test their limits.

"Djibouti!"

"The toilet!"

Clearly, I would need to establish some rules next time we sang this song. After about twenty times through the chorus, I was pretty sure they would never forget it.

The end of our jam session came quickly. Before anyone was ready to stop, we had to pack up the guitar and start our math lesson. The students from Linda's class who came to me for math were already starting to line up outside my door. They peeked in as we finished the last round of the chorus. No one said anything, but I know they were wondering whether or not my Singing Teacher alter ego would emerge again during math class.

I put the guitar away and secretly grew anxious for the next time we would get to sing together again.

At some point during the middle of the school year, I realized my discipline plan of calling out students for every misdeed was not sustainable. Once again, I really only had the outdated discipline methods used by my own teachers to draw from, so it felt as if I was continually improvising as I encountered everything from minor disruptions to outright defiance. Complicating this issue was the fact I had never needed much classroom discipline as a child—I mostly sat quietly at my desk and did what I was told—so I never got to know my teachers' classroom management strategies up close and personal.

After a particularly challenging week of annoying behavior from my students, I had the realization my classroom was probably not a very enjoyable place to be for several hours each day. From a student's perspective, I imagined my endless stream of "Don't do that!" and "Hey, stop!" and "Um, we're waiting for you!" was nothing more than an annoying swarm of word gnats, whiny and ornery and better off somewhere else. What kid would want to be in a class where the teacher barks negativity at the students all day? If I was miserable, so were the students.

This is when a *deus ex machina* moment occurred right before my eyes. I had been rummaging around in the fourth-grade supply closet looking for a set of math manipulatives to use the next day, and I came across a thin box with the words "Fraction Set" across the front in bold, colorful letters. I opened it up to find two sets of thick cardboard fraction pieces—⅛, ¼, ½, ¾—and a whole circle. One set was solid colors, with each fraction represented by a different hue. The other set looked like a pizza.

Just like that, another idea: What if I had a way of catching the students being good rather than nitpicking them all day? I began to craft this strategy in my head, and by the beginning of the next week I had a plan. Each time I caught the class, or an individual student, doing something good I would give the class a pizza slice. As they earned more slices,

I would replace the slices with larger fraction equivalents. You know, two ⅛ pieces was equal to ¼, and so on. It was like BOGO at the bakery, where you buy one iced cookie and get an oatmeal cookie for free. I was reinforcing good behavior *and* fraction skills at the same time.

I bought some magnetic strip tape and stuck a couple of pieces to each fraction slice so they would cling to the metal whiteboard in front of my room. All of the pieces were stacked in the pen tray at the base of the whiteboard, ready to go when class started the next week.

Monday arrived, and early on in the day I put a ⅛ piece on the board without saying anything. One of the students blurted out, "What's that for? Are we having a pizza party?"

"No, this is a new idea I have. Each time I catch the class, or even just one student, doing something good, I'll give you a pizza slice. If another teacher gives our class a compliment, you get a slice. If everyone comes in from recess without arguing or having to be reminded what to do next, you get a slice. If you are able to earn the whole pizza by the end of the week, we will spend some time doing something fun.

"What if we do something bad? Do we lose a piece?"

I predicted they would ask this. By the fourth grade, these kids knew when rewards were being held over their heads, or in some cases held against them. I wanted this strategy to be different.

"We all make mistakes or do stuff we know we shouldn't do. Those mistakes shouldn't undo the good things we have done. If a teacher gives you a compliment, who am I to take it away? We should be able to learn from mistakes, not let them undo the progress we have made."

"What kind of fun stuff do we get to do on Friday?"

"I will make a poster with some options. We can play a class game, get some extra reading time from our book, or I may get out the guitar and we can sing some songs together." When I said the word "guitar," the entire class did a fist pump in silent celebration. I may have heard a few of them whisper-yell, "Yes!"

"What if we don't get the whole circle?"

"Well, then you get another opportunity next week to earn the whole pizza." My mission was clear. I had to be alert enough during the week to catch the class being good eight times. Some weeks were more of a challenge than others, but I was convinced that finding eight instances of goodness was more about my mindset than it was their behavior.

As a final reminder, I told them the rules of the game. Once they earned a pizza slice, it was theirs for the week. No taking away pieces. Second, there was no *quid pro quo* or bargaining with the pizza slices. I would not promise a pizza slice in exchange for good behavior, and they couldn't make a pizza slice a condition for good behavior.

As predicted, the class earned their whole pizza by Thursday afternoon, which meant we would choose an activity from the Friday Fun Board. What I didn't predict was how Friday would become a celebration for our little community. The children celebrated making it to Friday, and I celebrated seeing the good in my students throughout the week. Honestly, I could have had thirty-six fraction pieces and it wouldn't have been enough. This strategy may have impacted the student's behavior, but I know for sure it affected mine.

It only took about two weeks for this event to be known universally as Friday Funday. I once overheard one of my students tell someone in another class, ". . . and if we get the whole pizza, we do fun stuff *all day* on Friday." Maybe fifteen minutes of uninterrupted fun feels like an entire day, but I promise I found time for the spelling test.

## CHAPTER 12 *Proxy*

LINDA AND CAROL SAVED ME. The visit to the teacher store was the first of countless acts of kindness and support they showed me throughout the years. As my own mother worried about me from a thousand miles away, these two ladies served as a proxy for her, shepherding me through some of the hardest, most emotional days of my life.

When an angry parent showed up one day at my door about an hour after school ended, unloading one grievance after another, they were waiting for me when she left. I found out later Carol stood outside my door, out of sight, listening to every word, ready to intervene if the mom got hostile. They helped me separate the parent's criticisms of my teaching from her deeply personal comments. Comments about my intelligence, my lack of personal qualities expected of an educator, her belief that Texas had enough problems without also having to give jobs to another state's bad teachers. The truth was, I was inexperienced and just about every aspect of my teaching was messy, but I was also languishing due to so many life changes at once. They helped me understand how parents many times will displace their frustration or discouragement with their child, their situation, or life in general on teachers or administrators. My mind was still a flurry of her harsh words, flying in every direction with no logic, no meaning, no predictable pattern. Each word had her face, swirling around me screaming and pointing, obscuring everything else around me.

"That really sucked." Carol and Linda gave me the space to talk through what happened, to start processing my emotions. More importantly, they assured me that being a teacher meant there was always the potential for these kinds of interactions, even when things seemed to be going well. They also reminded me how some parents were more likely to chew out a new teacher, and the longer I taught the less likely these types of confrontations were to happen.

One day as I was driving home from work, my old Chevy Blazer began to sputter and cough, and eventually it died about three exits from my apartment. My ability to troubleshoot computers was almost perfectly counterbalanced by my inability to know what to do if my car stopped working. My first indication that something was wrong came when my S-10 Blazer lurched and began to slow. I was in the center lane toward the end of rush hour, and I felt a compulsion to keep up with the traffic. I lifted my right foot off the gas pedal and pressed it down again a couple of times to see if the engine was responding. Nothing. The truck continued to slow down, and I knew if I didn't get to the right shoulder soon, I would be stranded in the center of the highway. My pulse began to race as I thought about coasting across two lanes of traffic, and my heart continued pounding in my chest when I pulled over. My natural response was to pop the hood and stare at the engine, which is what I did for about two minutes. Since I didn't drive a Transformer or Herbie the Lovebug, my truck was incapable of speaking to tell me what was wrong.

I grew up in Wyoming and have been lost in the wilderness on my mountain bike. I have gotten lost in Outlaw Canyon while fishing with my dad in the Bighorn Mountains. I have delivered newspapers at 5 a.m. during a blinding snowstorm and been chased by an angry (or aggressively playful) dog for three blocks. I have driven across Wyoming and Utah in blizzards traveling to and from college. Each of these events was horrifying, but none of them came close to the fear I felt when I was stranded on the side of the highway in an unfamiliar city with a broken-down truck somewhere on the outskirts of Fort Worth.

The cars and trucks buzzed within inches of my truck in a high-pitched whir at what seemed like a million miles per hour. Each semi-truck that flew by created a gust of hot wind that made me unsteady on my feet, forcing me to regain my balance.

This was the first time I had ever had a vehicle break down on me. I had run out of gas before, but that was my own stupid fault, and I was in a town small enough to walk to a gas station and borrow a gas can. I had no prior experience to help me figure this out. I scanned up and down the access road for a place that might have a phone. I could see a gas station in the distance, so I grabbed my book bag, locked the doors, and scampered down the hill leading to the access road. The bell on the door jingled as I pushed it open, and I asked the attendant sitting behind the counter if I could borrow a phone book and their phone. I thumbed through the yellow pages of the thick book until I found what I believed to be Carol's number. I punched in the numbers, and her husband Freddy answered. I had only met him one other time when he came by the school to drop something off for Carol, but I took a breath deep enough to explain my dilemma. He asked which highway I was on and told me he would be there as quickly as he could. I had called in the middle of their supper.

Carol and Freddy lived a little over thirty minutes from where my Blazer was stranded. In that amount of time, I had been able to call a tow truck, which arrived at almost the same time as they did. The man in the wrecker loaded up my car and asked me where to take it, which turned out to be another question I was unprepared to answer. Freddy told him the name and location of a good mechanic not too far from my apartment, and we followed him in their car. Carol and Freddy waited outside in their car while the receptionist at the auto shop filled out the ticket with my contact information.

It was almost 9 p.m. when they dropped me off at my apartment, and Carol told me what time she would be there to get me in the morning. After another thirty-minute drive home, she would do it again in less than ten hours. This experience was humbling, and I felt ashamed for having ruined this family's evening. Their son was a freshman in high school, which meant he probably had to finish dinner on his own and was waiting for his parents to return. Dejected, I walked up the stairs to my apartment and rummaged through my pantry and refrigerator for something to eat. There were no restaurants within walking distance of my apartment. Despite this turn of bad luck, I crunched on Frosted Mini-Wheats in silence with deep feelings of gratitude. I had someone willing to drop what they were doing and help me in my time of need.

When I walked into the school in late February on my birthday, I was pretty sure I was the only one who knew, and I believed there was nothing to celebrate. I secretly thought, *If I could just make it through the day without any major episodes from the usual suspects, I would accept that as a pretty good birthday gift.* As predicted, no one said a word to me about my birthday for the better part of the day. As I was lining my class up to take them to lunch, Carol stuck her head in my door and asked, "After you drop your kids off, could you drop by my room for a minute? I need help with something."

When I walked into her room for what I thought was a quick question, I was holding my sack lunch. I saw Linda and Carol sitting at the back table, which had been transformed into a dining room, complete with place settings, glasses, and a crockpot of something that smelled better than anything I had cooked for myself since moving to Texas. I knew at once what it was for. I had to fight back tears as I walked past the student desks toward the birthday celebration I never suspected. We gathered in the back of Carol's classroom and ate chicken and dumplings, told stories, and laughed a lot. When I first joined them at the table, they only had one rule: We couldn't talk about work.

As we finished our meal and the time to go retrieve our classes drew near, Linda reached under her chair and handed me a package covered in birthday-themed wrapping paper. I was reminded once again that Carol and Linda weren't just teachers. They were wives and mothers with a house, people waiting for them when they returned home, and somewhere in their homes was a place where they stored supplies for wrapping gifts. I knew exactly where that place was in my parent's house, and I envisioned Carol or Linda reaching into a closet or under a bed to retrieve colorful paper and bows. If they were anything like my mom, they used the guest bed as an ad hoc table. The place where you store wrapping paper represents kindness, thoughtfulness, the place where you go when you want to do something special for someone. It's the middle stop between buying and giving, and in the midst of their busy lives as teachers and moms and wives, they took time away to do something nice for the new kid, and they wrapped it in a bow. For the second time that day, I had to pretend I was yawning to help relax the lump that was building in my throat.

The gift was a book, which I kind of predicted based on the size and weight of the package. It was a biography of a man who struggled to find himself early in life. He stumbled half-asleep through one experience after another, leaving behind a trail of broken pieces: relationships, goals, opportunities. It wasn't until much later in his life that he looked back and realized all the broken pieces created a beautiful mosaic, each one an irreplaceable tile in the story of his life. A fitting story indeed for a guy currently standing in the midst of a few broken pieces himself.

## CHAPTER 13 Imposter

*Children moving about the room, avoiding eye contact.*

*Fuzzy watching.*

*Always watching.*

FUZZY CONTINUED TO DISPLAY AGGRESSIVE and erratic behavior for the next few weeks. He rarely left his miniature hamster hut, the former residence of the hamster I assumed this imposter had murdered in cold blood before stuffing him behind a shoe in the closet and slipping quietly into his new life as a classroom pet. He would occasionally climb into the running wheel in his cage, but he wouldn't run. He walked just fast enough to maximize the squeak in the wheel. And he would wait until the perfect moment when the squeaking of the wheel would cause the most distraction among the children, like during a math lesson or silent reading. I would look over the heads of my students toward the cage, and there was Fuzzy walking steadily, staring at me the whole time. His eyes told the story, "What are you going to do about it? Go ahead, reach your hand in here and stop me."

Life in the classroom continued like this for a couple of months with the new Fuzzy. The student project, as well as my free pet care, basically came to a stop. Students who used to stop and ogle Fuzzy and speak to him in a high-pitched voice now just passed by without so much as turning their heads. No one asked to hold him. There were no requests to put him in his ball to roll around the room, so the children could giggle as he bumped into chairs and desks. I had a routine of filling his water and giving him food each evening before I left to go home because none of the children would go near his cage. To be honest, I think Fuzzy liked it that way.

Somewhere around mid-January, the imposter actually escaped. I came in one morning and found the door open and the cage empty. I was already running late, so I didn't have time to launch a full-scale search party. I looked in some of the obvious areas where I thought he might be hiding: under the desks, in my supply closet, and in the bookshelves. After a few minutes of half-hearted searching around the classroom, I knew I needed to get things ready for the day ahead. My percipient students noticed he was not in his cage as they paraded into the classroom.

"Mr. Alexander, you know Fuzzy's not in his cage, right?" This was spoken in the same casual tone a student may have used to inform me the shavings in the pencil sharpener needed to be emptied.

No one seemed upset or displayed any urgency to find him. In the couple months the new Fuzzy had been in our classroom, his vibe was clearly that of someone who came and went from his cage as he darn well pleased.

I alerted the school staff of our escapee and, because of his nocturnal tendencies, asked the custodial staff to keep an eye out for him. A few days later, he was in his cage with the door closed, and none of the custodians knew who found him and put him back in his cage. I pictured Fuzzy rowing across a hazy hidden lake beneath the school, referring to himself as the Angel of Music.

By the time March arrived, I had almost forgotten there was a list of names on a sheet of paper with corresponding dates for when students would take Fuzzy home for the weekend. Our class book only had about twelve entries, and I was beginning to surrender to the idea of sending home a flat paper hamster with the students who had not yet contributed to the project just so I could have a journal page for each child. My only consolation in this entire debacle was being a first-year teacher, a verified rookie in every sense. I had been told repeatedly during college to expect bumps and hiccups during my first year of teaching. This is a hard job, and no one, not even that one person in my Science Methods class who had every assignment done four weeks in advance and retyped the notes from every lecture, would escape the first year without some "teachable moments," forward fails, and other clichés they tell newbies who feel like idiots.

I guess this is why I was a little stunned when Daniel asked me if he was still allowed to take Fuzzy home for the weekend. I had already labeled the project a bust.

"Are you sure you want to do this, Daniel? I mean, most of the other kids in the class have backed out. To be honest, Fuzzy kind of gives me the creeps."

"Well, I signed up at the beginning of the year, and I've been waiting for my turn for a long time. My mom says it's okay, and I really want to take him home."

It's your death sentence, Daniel. "If that's what you want, you are certainly welcome to take Fuzzy home. I'll make sure you have all the supplies you need." May the power of Grayskull be with you, Daniel.

Friday afternoon arrived, and Daniel gleefully trotted out of my classroom with his backpack, the bag full of supplies, and Fuzzy in his cage. For the first time since I began this class project, I was not worried for the hamster. Daniel, on the other hand, was in my thoughts and prayers. I fully expected to come to work on Monday to the news my student and his family had been attacked in their sleep. One tiny bite at a time.

The following Monday, I was walking through the cafeteria toward the teacher's lounge to put my lunch in the refrigerator when I saw Daniel sitting on the steps leading up to the stage. I slowed my pace slightly and asked Daniel how the weekend went. He had a sheepish look on his face.

"Well, Mr. Alexander, things didn't go so well."

"Oh no, Daniel, did Fuzzy bite you?" Did your little brother chase his paper airplane and try to retrieve it from Fuzzy's cage, only to pull back a bloody nub where his arm used to be?

"No, he didn't bite me. I didn't even get a chance to take him out of the cage. When I got home, my mom took one look at Fuzzy and told me there was no way that animal was staying in our house. She made me put him outside in my fort, and when I went out the next morning to check on him, he was gone."

I imagined a group of neighbors all standing in their driveways, talking across their shrubs. They were discussing the mysterious disappearance of dozens of house cats. I wonder if there was a noticeable drop in the squirrel population. Did the air seem suddenly more still, eerily quiet with fewer birds singing?

"Mr. Alexander, I am really sorry about losing Fuzzy. I don't know how it happened. My mom felt so bad about it. She called some of the neighbors, and one of them had a hamster who just had babies, and they gave me one. I've been calling him Tarzan because he likes to climb all over the cage."

"Daniel, this is totally not your fault. We already knew Fuzzy knew how to escape from his cage, and I guess he just really wanted to be free." Words cannot express the wave of relief and elation that swept through my entire body, and I had to use every acting skill I acquired during my one year as a musical theatre major to pretend I was sympathizing with the guilt Daniel was feeling.

"Well, he's a cutie, I'll give him that. Tarzan, you say. Thanks for being honest about this, Daniel." Unlike *some* people! "It may have been Fuzzy's time to be free, and I think the other kids will be happy to meet Tarzan. I'm heading back to the classroom, so I can take our new friend with me."

The kids recognized the new hamster almost immediately when they came into the class that day.

"Mr. Alexander, thank you so much for finally getting a different hamster! That other one really freaked me out."

I explained to the class how Fuzzy had escaped his cage over the weekend, and Daniel was able to get a new hamster for us during our time of loss. Not one child in the room even tried to act sad. The excitement was visible as children began asking if they could hold him (they always assumed it was a male), who would be the first to feed him, and most importantly, the children were once again interested in taking him home. I had always been told the best way to get attention was to show up with a baby or a puppy, and I guess the same was true for baby hamsters.

"Wait! If Fuzzy ran away, are we going to call this hamster Fuzzy, too?"

Daniel told the class about the name he had chosen, and no one liked it. For the second time that year, everyone put their heads down on their desks to vote on a name for the new hamster. Technically, had I not let Scotty off the hook, this should have been the third vote. Everyone made suggestions, we voted, and within a few minutes we had a name: Pete.

It didn't take us long to figure out how Daniel came up with Pete's original name, Tarzan. He loved to climb all over the inside of the cage and swing from the ceiling. Just like Fuzzy had the gift of hijacking the children's attention at the worst times, Pete was developing his own skill set in this area. Just as I would be making a dramatic point in the social studies lesson or demonstrating the most important step in a math operation, a child would glance back at Pete's cage and announce to the whole class, "Look! Pete is hanging upside down!" Before I could make an empty threat, the whole class would be out of their seats huddled around his cage, making affectionate high-pitched sounds, motioning for me to come see.

Over time, these acrobatic aerials became commonplace, and I was again able to teach a full lesson without Pete distracting everyone in the room. I imagine this did not sit well with Pete, and he may have begun to imagine ways to redirect attention back toward himself. When you think about it, a hamster has limited options for engaging an audience. First of all, I am pretty sure the natural tendency of a one-ounce rodent in the wild is to attract as little attention as possible. From a survival standpoint, it is in the rodent's favor to make sure every hawk, owl, or fox in the vicinity doesn't know you are there. There is no way for a socialized domestic pet raised in captivity to understand this.

Other than hanging from the cage, Pete's options were, in no particular order:

> Being cute, but kids are surrounded by cuteness all the time and it's a jungle out there.

Running on the wheel, but Fuzzy the Deceiver had already desensitized the class to that gimmick.

Squealing and squeaking, but hamsters have limited vocal ability, and from where the cage was positioned in the room, I doubt his vocalizations would even penetrate the human ear.

Playing dead, but even Pete wasn't this desperate.

I really had no idea what was going on in Pete's head or his process for solving problems, but I can tell you this, he came up with a dandy. Pete's new method for causing a ruckus in my classroom was probably more creative than any of my students could have come up with, and it was definitely more daring. Specifically, he would straddle the bars of the cage in the spread-eagle position and pee on the countertop. The first few times it happened I didn't even witness him in the act. I noticed the drops of water around the cage and assumed one of my students spilled a little when filling his water bottle. A few days later, I actually saw him do it, but none of the students could see because they were facing me and their backs were to the cage. It took me a minute to process what had just happened, but when I saw the same little puddle on the countertop, I made the connection. I was once again the only person to see the third occurrence of this vile attention grab, but my reaction must have been remarkable because every student stared at me, then looked to see what I was staring at. The entire class turned their heads just in time to see Pete finish his business. The class fizzed over in a cascade of shrieks and groans, and a few of the students even raced over to see the mess. I swear to this day Pete was smiling at me.

From that day on, the children subconsciously coordinated their efforts to make sure at least one person was monitoring Pete's cage at all times. I laid an old towel under his cage, doing my best to make sure the edge of the towel extended beyond his estimated projection capabilities. If Pete was as smart as I gave him credit for, he would eventually start holding his pee for longer periods in order to increase the distance he could launch his rage. From that point on, anytime I would hear even a slight disturbance in my classroom noise level, I would immediately look at the hamster cage. And as if on cue, I would see Pete clinging to the cage and a small stream of entertainment gold forming an arc toward the surface of the counter. Pete would smile or occasionally wink at me.

The first few moments after the children left school at the end of the day brought a welcome serenity to the classroom. For many days, this would be the first time since lunch I had even sat down. This was before social media and smartphones, so I partitioned off this time in the day to take a few deep breaths and gather my thoughts. I might sort through a stack of student papers or organize the top of my desk. As I shuffled and rearranged papers, I glanced toward the direction of Pete's cage and saw him drinking from his water bottle. He paused to look through the bars back at me, whiskers twitching as he gave his paws a spit bath.

Both Pete and I were strangers in this place, displaced into a foreign land. Our surroundings were not what we were accustomed to and probably not what either of us envisioned in a time gone by when we used to dream about the future. Pete may have even had an advantage over me because he didn't really contemplate his surroundings or purpose in life. I was alone in that pursuit.

"We're both imposters, pal."

> Imposter
>
> Outsider
>
> Unqualified
>
> Poser
>
> Fake
>
> Wannabe
>
> Misfit
>
> Hack

Unspoken words, uttered to myself over and over, swirling in my head. This was not my first encounter with imposter syndrome. During my first year of college while studying theatre, I was cast in Peter Shaffer's *Amadeus* as Baron van Swieten. My limited experience in theatre up to this point had mainly involved young, starry-eyed comedic characters in musicals, and this was the first time I had been given a serious role. Baron van Swieten was a politician and patron of the arts who funded Mozart's career as a composer and helped get him inducted into the Masons. The baron was somewhere between forty-five and fifty-five years old, and putting me in this role as a nineteen-year-old felt like an egregious miscasting. Despite the hours I put into rehearsal, learning my lines, and trying to get into character, Baron van Swieten never fit right. I was used to getting a response from the audience—laughter and applause—and being met with silence was torture. In my character's final interaction with Mozart, I cut him off from his lone source of financial support, leaving him at the mercy of the masked stranger commissioning his final work, *Requiem*. My final lines in the play left Mozart whimpering and the audience in stunned silence. Yet, the void left me more concerned with whether or not the audience liked me than if I had faithfully played this key part in the story. Whatever talent I may have had as an actor was contaminated by my immature craving for instant gratification. This experience led me to question my future as a theatre performer.

Teaching had its own form of silence, and I once again found myself caught between the tension of being the star of the show and a key part of the story. The progression through elementary school and the world of gold stars and participation ribbons into the GPA and class-ranking system of high school had been relatively painless. Leaving high school for college just meant swapping the honor roll for the dean's list and class rank for one of the "cum laude" designations. Up to this point in my life, there had always been a tangible, expected recognition of my efforts. As a teacher, I experienced a recognition vacuum, and I was more likely to be scolded than praised.

Just like Pete, I found myself stretching for ways to be validated. There was the time I sent home a survey to the parents in order to receive feedback on my teaching up to that point. Of the surveys that came back, a couple were positive, several were negative, and one was covered in red proofreading marks. Don't forget the lame jokes throughout the day, derailing any progress we were making toward actual learning goals. I remember attempting a wisecrack in a faculty meeting, forgetting I was sitting in a school library and not a fraternity house. The only response I got was from a colleague who barked, "Oh, Curby, just grow up!" A more constructive practice was when I would read to the class or play songs on my guitar, a reliable source of smiles and laughter. I learned quickly as a teacher, you better appreciate those rare moments of unsolicited praise, feedback, or encouragement.

The need for external praise eventually gave way to a more stable reliance on internal motivators. I eventually learned the value of setting grading goals and reaching them before Friday, so I could spend time with friends without guilt. I prioritized certain tasks so I could be available to stand at the door of my classroom and greet my students by name as they arrived at school. Most importantly, I learned to have faith in myself, to trust the efficacy of these small rewards at leaving a lasting impact.

Pete and I, two strangers learning to adapt to new surroundings, a new metaphysical ecosystem of purpose and function. Would Pete ever become content with his adorable fuzziness and nothing else? Could I find peace in a job well done? I couldn't speak for Pete, but for this class clown it was worth the effort.

For months, we had been focused on preparing our students for the state reading, math, and writing test. The shelf behind my desk was littered with worksheets, practice tests, and samples of the students' writing. The frenetic madhouse of testing at the end of the year eventually gave way to more student-centered projects. Test review worksheets were replaced with projects the students enjoyed. They made dioramas of their favorite geographic landforms using half a shoe box, dirt from their yard, twigs from trees, and other supplies they could find at home. Students took passages from their favorite books and transformed them into reader's theatre, which they performed for the class using silly voices, dialogue, and ad hoc costumes from home. We played kickball, sang songs, and pursued other fun activities we didn't dare try until the last test had been taken. The end of the school year also included traditions like field day and trips to the museum. Just when it seemed we were settling into a rhythm of fun and curiosity, the calendar reminded me we were starting the last week of school. Projects built from construction paper and items from the recycling bin were replaced with piles of forgotten papers and pencil nubs rescued from the depths of the students' desks. They sorted through their desks to separate the items belonging to the school from those they would take home for the summer. They scrubbed their desks inside and out until the scent of all-purpose cleaner permeated every corner of the room. Similar to the feverish start to the school year, the students and their supplies departed my classroom with anticipation for lazy mornings, camps, pool parties, and video games. All that remained was me standing among the stacks of textbooks. And yes, Pete found a new home for summer, which eventually became his permanent home.

My first year of teaching still stands as the most intense learning experience I have ever had, more than graduate school or becoming a parent. Every day, I was confronted with something new, or at least new enough that what I learned the day before still needed to be adapted in some way. One thing I learned about myself was pet ownership was not something I preferred to mix with my teaching. Teachers should bring their unique talents and passions into the classroom and share them with their students. Some teachers love art and crafts, others love music or fun games. And some teachers love keeping pets in the classroom, but I am not that teacher, so I found my own passions to enrich my classroom.

I've told the story of me and the hamsters countless times over the years, and people always want to know if I ever solved the mystery of the first Fuzzy. During my fourth year of teaching at Timberline, Scotty's younger sister Karleigh was a student in my class. Apparently, she had heard a few things about my class from her two older brothers who were my former students. She took pride in announcing to the class how she already knew the words to the songs we sang together or the next book we would read. Having vicariously experienced my class two times already, she became somewhat of an oracle for the other children. With my two hamsters now a distant memory, I never made the connection between Karleigh and the Fuzzies.

One day out of the blue, as the class was working quietly, a student asked, "Mr. Alexander, why don't you have any class pets like Mrs. Cate?"

"Well, I used to have a hamster, but he's no longer with us. I'll tell you about him some time."

Karleigh looked up from her book and replied in front of everyone, "Oh yeah, remember when my brother Scotty was in your class and he brought your hamster home and he died and we gave you one of our hamsters and you never found out?"

Well played, Scotty. Well played.

## CHAPTER 14 Communion

THE CHOICES KIDS HAVE FOR READING these days are astounding. When I was in elementary and middle school, there were not that many books, much less entire series, aimed exclusively at children. We had the *Little House* books by Laura Ingalls Wilder, the *Hardy Boys*, and, of course, there were the books by Judy Blume and Beverly Cleary, but none of those really got me excited to read. Other than reading nonfiction books about "strange and mysterious" facts, I preferred playing outside or re-creating adventures with my action figures over settling down to read for long stretches. I also liked TV, which didn't help my mom's efforts to get me to read more.

All of that changed when I started college. I read a lot in middle and high school, but it was mainly because my teachers assigned a lot of reading and I wanted to make good grades. Through brute force, I made myself read out of obligation rather than for enjoyment or personal improvement. My teachers assigned pages to read, and I made sure against all odds, at some point before the due date my eyes passed over those pages and more or less made sense of the words. The entire exchange was a transaction.

While sitting backstage at a rehearsal for a musical I was in, a friend I met through the production began talking about a book he was reading. He talked about the characters as if he knew them, the plot as one of his own experiences. I had never met someone who loved stories in this way. He loved books like I loved *Star Wars* and *Indiana Jones* when I was ten. He appreciated the art and sought it as an escape all at once. The next day, I drove to the mall between classes and bought one of the books he had talked about, and once I started reading, I was hooked.

Over the course of my first year as a teacher, I read about ten different books with my class. I started with one I had read before, *The Stone Fox*, the sad tale of a boy and his dog in Wyoming who race for their lives to win the prize money and save the family farm. In hindsight, this was probably not a great book to start with. I never envisioned ending my first full week as a teacher seeing half the class with tears streaming down their faces and wiping their runny noses on their sleeve. But that was how it shook down.

I decided to pick something a little more upbeat for the next book, so I went with *Watchdog and the Coyotes*. It was funny and gave me the opportunity to use different voices for each of the characters. You know, practice for my acting career in case teaching didn't work out. I can't remember the entire read-aloud playlist throughout the year, but I'm pretty sure we read *The Giver, Number the Stars, Upchuck and the Rotten Willy, The Wainscott Weasel, Maniac Magee, Frindle,* and my all-time favorite, *Matilda*.

Maybe it was out of tradition, maybe it was me mimicking what my teachers had done, or it could have just been muscle memory, but every day after I picked up my class from lunch recess I would read for ten or fifteen minutes from a chapter book before starting the lessons for the afternoon. For a struggling first-year teacher, this was easily the best part of my day. Years later, one of the students in my first class looked me up and sent me a kind email during Teacher Appreciation Week. She wanted me to know she read her all-time favorite book for the first time in my class. I was humbled by how easily my teaching—my words, actions, and decisions—were recalled in such detail so many years later, and I hoped what other students remembered when they reminisced about being in my class was equally kind and pleasant.

Over the course of that year, books and music became a sort of communion for me and my students, a sacrament where we shared laughter and imagination. Those fifteen minutes I was able to set aside here and there became our escape hatch, a portal to distant times in faraway lands, where we witnessed common people become heroes, a shy girl discover her superpower, or a young man carry the burden of history on his shoulders. We sang songs about traveling, about everyday items hiding in a closet, about verbs, and numbers, about ordinary events like picture day, and breaking classroom rules.

My struggles as a teacher early in my career, especially the first year, are no secret, but I never struggled with music or sharing stories with my students. In those moments, art was enough. There were no benchmarks or normative scores to remind me where my students stood compared to everyone else. I had mastery of this domain and did not need to be monitored or put on an improvement plan. No, in those moments, I had something to offer. I needed a lot of validation in those early years, but I was confident in my ability to create a family of learners, a community built around care and support. I shared music and stories directly from my heart to theirs, no filter or buffer.

When I look back on my years as a classroom teacher, I mostly think about the students. I remember chubby, freckled faces framed by fresh haircuts to start the school year. These memories stand in contrast to the students at the end of the year: slightly thinner faces with features more defined, a little more confident, a little less dependent on me. Their pants that are too short, shirts that are too big. I see their eyes light up and can hear the delighted murmurs start to rise when I would walk to the closet where I stored the guitar. The veins popping in their necks as their red faces strain to hit the high notes. Students smirking at each other across the room, temporarily linked by one of my silly lyrics. I hear them begging me, "Please, Mr. Alexander! You can't stop reading *there*! It's Friday . . . we have to know what happens! Please!" when I would get to the end of a chapter. Those moments were sacred. Word by word, note by note, stories, lyrics, and melodies were weaving my students' lives into mine and mine into theirs.

Years later when I had my own children, I decided to read them *Matilda*, one chapter each night before bed, just as I had done after lunch when I was a teacher. The moment I began reading, I was transported to the first time my eyes lifted Roald Dahl's words from the page. Every word carried the memory of precious years with my copilots from learning journeys long passed. For a few minutes each night, we were invited into the whimsical world of his imagination, and each time I awakened anew to the power of words colliding with the mind. Sometimes we would dim the lights or read by flashlight to immerse ourselves deeper into his world of words. As our small family of four huddled around the worn copy of the book I had kept all those years, we knew we were not alone. I would enter this sanctuary to read, but I dared not look up from the pages. If I had, I was certain to see a host of students, all looking at me anxiously, all waiting for what happens next.

## CHAPTER 15  *Busted*

MARK PROBABLY WISHED I HAD NEVER STEPPED into the hallway. I stuck my head out the door after school to tell him and some other boys to start heading home. This is when I noticed one of the boys in the group crying.

"Hey, guys, what's going on? Robert, are you okay?"

"No! Mark called me the P-word!" He melted into a puddle right there in front of his friends.

"Mark, is this true?" My mind raced through its Rolodex of cuss words as I tried to guess which P-word may have been used in this situation. There were a few to choose from.

"No, I didn't! I never called you anything!"

"He's lying!" Robert bawled. "You called me the P-word!"

"It was an accident!" Now both boys were crying uncontrollably. I decided not to probe Mark further about which of the P-words he had used. I was pretty sure he knew all of them.

"Don't go there, Mark. Words like that don't just come out by accident. We're going to have to talk to your parents about this." Mark's timing could not have been worse. Parent-teacher conferences were the next day, and his parents were my first conference after lunch. Mark would be coming with them.

The next day, the meeting with Mark's parents went about as well as you can expect a parent-teacher conference to go. We talked about his strengths, some areas of improvement, and I left time for some questions.

"Yes, I was just wondering how Mark's behavior has been."

Funny. You. Should. Ask.

"Well, Mark has his good and bad days, just like all of us. I haven't noticed anything extremely disruptive, and anytime he steps out of line I address it right away." Unlike my meeting with Colby's mom, I wasn't letting Mark off the hook. "He did have an incident the other day after school where he made a friend cry by calling him an inappropriate name. I don't know what word it was, but his friend was pretty upset."

In unison, both parents looked at their son sitting between them. "Oh really! Exactly what word did you say?"

"It was an accident! I don't want to say it in front of Mr. Alexander. I promise, I'll never say it again!"

"Oh no! If you can say it to a friend, you can say it right here." His mom had a missile lock on him, and she was taking no prisoners. "What word did you use?"

"Penis," Mark mumbled almost inaudibly at the tabletop.

What happened next could not have been scripted any better by the best screenwriter in Hollywood. For a moment, I felt transported into a parallel dimension where I was part of the audience in a live production of a parent-teacher conference.

Mark's parents both turned in their seats, hunched over their son, and yelled, "*What?*"

Mark's mom leaned back and began to recite what I believe to be some version of Hail Mary, Full of Grace. His dad, seemingly at a loss for words, just repeated, "Uh-uh, no way! No. Way. Uh-uh, *my* son does *not* talk like that! No way, no way. Uh-uh."

In real time, this probably lasted for fifteen seconds, tops, probably less. In my surreal dream world, it appeared to be playing on a repeating loop for eternity. I restrained myself from laughing at this comedic scene, knowing the personal agony Mark was currently experiencing. Glancing at the look on his face, it was clear he would've done just about anything to get out of this meeting. I had been in the same hot seat before, and it was awful. Just Mark and the truth and the purification that only comes from the fires of public parental scorn.

To put this in context, Mark had it coming. He was mouthy and sarcastic and mischievous and generally one of those students who would tattle on his classmates to get them in trouble then threaten to beat up the same kids if they ever snitched on him. I was able to keep Mark in line during class, so he reserved his best work for recess. His parents were mostly supportive, but they thought he was cute and sometimes treated him more like a friend than their child. In most cases, if any of his shenanigans at school made it into a note home or a phone call, there would be more excuses than consequences. Too much sugar, too little sleep, too much TV and video games, not enough time outside. He'd be on good behavior for a while, then the whole cycle would start over in a couple of days. Mark wasn't a total disruption, but he was a sneaky little agitator. All his little annoyances had been somehow stored up in a big ball of karma, and they all came back on him at once. I scanned back and forth between his mom and his dad as they read him the Riot Act, occasionally dipping my gaze as I passed between them just to see him squirm.

"We are so sorry about this, Mr. Alexander. It won't happen again, will it, Mark?"

"No, ma'am."

"Thank you for coming in. See you tomorrow, Mark."

"Yes, sir." He never looked up as he slowly marched out the door between his parents. Whether he learned anything from the experience I don't know, but Mark got a dose of accountability that day and he learned his parents and I were allies. Some lessons are just so personally offensive.

During my years as a teacher, I had thousands of interactions with parents. Most of them were polite and amiable, sometimes they were humorous or heartbreaking, and they rarely turned hostile. The cumulative effect of these exchanges gave me insight into peaks and valleys that come with parenthood.

I have tried to comfort a parent who was grieving over the death of a teenage child, desperately trying to hold her family together in the face of tragedy.

I have read piles of handwritten notes hastily scratched on everything from napkins to receipts. Notes asking me to excuse a child's absence because "she had a touch of pneumonia," or "Please don't call me at work. I *know* his homework isn't done! It's my fault!" I was sometimes told I gave too much homework and "If I am expected to teach my child math, then I might as well quit my job and become a teacher!" or "You're the teacher. Do your job!"

I have cheered alongside parents at soccer, baseball, and basketball games on Saturday mornings.

I once visited a student and his mother at their home the day after the sudden passing of her husband. Helpless and distraught, we just sat together and wept.

I have passed the tissue box to a single father as he tried to process the news about his son's learning disability. Through his tears he told everyone in the meeting, "I always hoped my son wouldn't struggle in school like I did. It's the worst feeling, being forced to do something day in and day out when everyone thinks you're dumb."

I received phone calls at home, asking me why I assigned a class project that morning when it was due the next day. The project that was assigned three weeks prior. The project for which they had signed the paper with the due date and the grading rubric. I would nod and avoid trying to defend myself. "Yes, I understand . . . Yes, I will accept it late. I agree, this is a good lesson about planning ahead and not procrastinating."

I've laughed along with parents about funny things their children have said or done, celebrated their victories, found joy in their achievements.

It's strange when you think about it, being surrounded by other people's children all day long. I always called my students "my kids," even though I was really only acting *in loco parentis*. In place of the parent, five days a week for 180 days, seven hours each day. That's a lot of time to spend with someone, then they suddenly move on whether you accomplished what you needed to or not.

To all the parents whose kids I have taught, I worked hard to be a good steward of the time we had together. I know I made a lot of mistakes, made comments I wish I could take back, forgot events I should have remembered, overlooked or brushed off behaviors that should have been addressed. I also saw them grow and learn. I saw them toil and get frustrated and stick with a task and never give up until they got it right. I watched them become more and more independent, needing me a little less each day. I could only imagine how you felt as their parents, cherishing every moment but unable to escape the faint, relentless ticking of time always in the background.

In some ways, we experienced the peaks and valleys together. Your children made me . . .

- Tired
- Energized
- Infuriated
- Whimsical
- Anxious
- Peaceful
- Nostalgic
- Hopeful
- Disappointed
- Proud
- Scattered
- Stable
- Driven
- Motivated
- Obsessed
- Perfectionistic
- Confused
- Annoyed
- Joyful
- Fulfilled.

They made me a teacher.

## CHAPTER 16 *Repaired*

WHEN THE SCHOOL YEAR ENDED in late May, Carol, Linda, and I met at Carol's house to do some planning for the next year. The school district had decided to renovate and expand our school, which meant we had to move out for one year. We had two weeks after the last day of school to pack up every item in our classrooms so the movers could take them to our temporary home, one wing of a middle school across the street. We could have met at the school, but it was crowded with boxes and most of the furniture had already been moved. From one box to many. My life, like the number of boxes sitting in my classroom, had grown exponentially.

After a long morning of planning and talking, we took a break for lunch. Beyond their friendship and the endless wealth of teaching advice, which I continually relied upon, my favorite part of working with Carol and Linda was the home-cooked meals. I don't even remember what we ate that day, but at least it wasn't from McDonald's or out of a can. At some point during the meal, Carol reached back and grabbed a gift bag and handed it to me. The memory of how they had gone out of their way to remember me three months earlier on my birthday was still fresh in my mind, and I was certainly not expecting any more presents. They both held back smiles as they watched me pull out the colored tissue paper and set it aside. In the bottom of the bag was a navy-blue T-shirt, and the front of it was covered in iron-on letters. The letters were arranged in a pattern resembling a crossword puzzle. As I studied the letters more closely, I realized each across and down was a different acronym from the year before: TEKS, TAAS, EXCET, IEP, ESL, and so on. I guess Carol and Linda understood how entering a new profession is like learning a new language, and that included all the jargon and acronyms that went along with it. I still have that T-shirt, though I don't think I ever actually wore it out of concern the letters might come off. It is still wrapped in a ziplock bag in my closet.

Carol and Linda had been there for every victory and setback during my four years at Timberline: buying a new truck, my futile attempts at finding a girlfriend, winning 5K races, the death of both great-grandmothers in a two-week span, and getting accepted into graduate school. We celebrated when things went well. We offered each other support when one of us was mistreated or experienced misfortune. They watched me grow and mature into a confident, capable teacher, eventually trusting me with grade-level responsibilities like planning field trips, designing student projects, writing and directing the fourth-grade musical, and eventually becoming the lead teacher.

The school year ended with no fanfare. My students were moving on to fifth grade, and their parents were probably relieved to be getting a new teacher. As I methodically progressed through the items on my end-of-year checklist, I was already daydreaming of driving north to spend part of the summer in Wyoming with my parents.

The day after I arrived home, I drove my dad's truck up Casper Mountain and down the canyon road to our family cabin. I unlocked the door, opened the windows to air out the stale miasma of the sealed-off cabin, and hiked down the canyon toward Elkhorn Creek. I had mentally escaped to my beloved canyon dozens of times throughout the year. I would imagine the smell of lodgepole pines, the sound of the creek rushing below, the sensation of wildflowers brushing up against my legs as I quickly skipped between and over fallen trees, granite boulders, and patches of grass. I would meditate upon the dry, clean air, and the hairs on my arms would quiver from the abrupt transition caused by hiking in and out of the shade from the canopy hanging over my head. One second

I was warmed by the rays of the sun at 8,600 feet elevation, and then it would dissipate into a cool embrace as I left its glow.

For the first time in many months, I did not have to imagine this moment. I was here surrounded by a place I loved, welcomed home by the quake of the aspens and song of the meadowlarks. Once I reached the creek, I had three options. The trail upstream was mostly flat with few obstacles, dotted with small pools filled by the water rolling over smooth, round rocks. If you knew where to look, you could sneak up on the pools and see brook trout resting in the middle of the current for an afternoon nap. Heading downstream was a little more technical, where the creek was juxtaposed by dense willow thickets blanketing its banks, sheer rock faces, and piles of debris from a flood many years ago. In some cases, all three terranean variations converged at once, at which point it was best to head to high ground and navigate around the obstacle course. The reward of heading downstream was a large, multi-tiered waterfall boxed in by massive rock formations on every side, a geological wonder completely unknown by all but a handful of people.

The third option was to keep hiking up the other side of the canyon, which is what I did. The grade of the incline was steep and soft from generations of pine needles covering the ground, which added an element of unpredictability to the already strenuous climb. My attempts to stay fit through jogging and cycling were quickly put to the test, and I pushed through the burning in my thighs to prove I could still reach the top of the canyon without stopping. A quick water break gave me a minute to appreciate the landscape stretched before me. I was now higher than my cabin, which now looked like a miniature model perched on top of some rocks. To my left was a vast expanse of lodgepole pine for miles and miles. To my right, the steep walls of the canyon framed the infinite prairie stretching north toward Montana.

Not wanting to waste time, I snapped the lid on my water bottle and ventured into the woods. Within minutes, I saw the first crack in the earth.

A crack in the earth. A fault. I guess I had more in common with my revered canyon than I realized. If the previous year of teaching had accomplished anything, it had revealed my faults. I had spent the last year consumed by the belief I had slipped through the cracks in my teacher training. The signs of my incompetence were there all along, but no one noticed them. Maybe someone saw them from the beginning and just didn't care enough to invest the necessary time to help me improve. Possibly, my faults, like these cracks in the mountain, had been there too long and were too big to do anything about.

I pushed past my thoughts and descended deeper into the woods. The fault lines became bigger and more frequent until I emerged onto a bald rock face on the edge of the canyon wall. On one side was a drop-off, perhaps five hundred or more feet. On the other side, about fifty yards from the cliff, was a gash in the rock about one hundred yards across. The fault was deep and littered with rock fragments left behind with nowhere to go.

Had there been a traumatic event that tore the mountain apart? An earthquake or volcanic activity? Violent enough to leave a gaping scar, but lacking the strength to lacerate the entire sheet of rock from the side of the gorge. Or had the crack slowly cleaved along a small fissure for thousands or millions of years? Season upon season of rain, snow, and ice, slowly exploiting its vulnerability, making way for more rain, snow, and ice in subsequent winters.

I wondered the same about myself. Within less than three months I graduated, moved, left my friends, started a new career, and began living on my own. So much change was traumatic and peeled away too much of my former life at once, leaving a deep fracture in my identity, all that I had ever known.

There was also the possibility these faults were there all along, deepening, widening steadily over time, and my circumstances forced me to confront them for the first time in my life. Did it even matter how my faults were exposed, as long as I was willing to either address them or learn to live with them?

I walked along the edge of the fault, looking for a place suitable to hop in and explore. The years of my youth were spent exploring spots up and down the canyon just like this one. I had been to this fault line dozens of times, climbed into its deep crevasses, scaled along its rough walls, under and over boulders wedged between the walls of the crack in the earth. The belly of the cavern was cool and shaded from the intense sun. Even late into the summer, I could find patches of snow hiding from summer's gaze, cold and mottled with dirt and pine needles blown in by the unrelenting Wyoming wind.

After exploring the crevasses and caverns for a little while, I hopped around between boulders on the surface of the fault line. This was when I began to notice something I had probably overlooked hundreds of times before. As I peered into the space between the rubble, I could see life emerging from the cracks. Streaks of wildflowers, pine saplings, a variety of grasses. As I took a step back and changed my focus, the boulders looked like towering peaks surrounded by ancient forests and valleys. In the midst of destruction, life had surfaced and made its home among the wreckage. Perhaps in another one hundred years or so, the fault wouldn't even be noticeable. Hikers would come to what they assumed was just another low spot in the forest without considering the forces that shaped its contours.

The Japanese art of *kintsugi* translates to mean "golden joinery," although some people call it *kintsukuroi*, or "golden repair." Artists who have mastered this form take broken everyday objects like bowls, plates, and saucers, and they mend the breakage with liquid gold, silver, or platinum. The end result is beautiful. The philosophy behind this artform is to honor the breakage and subsequent repair as part of each item's history rather than disguising the cracks and treating them as something that should be forgotten. This aligns with the broader Japanese philosophy of *wabi-sabi*, which is the embracing of change, flaws, and imperfections. The cracks tell part of a beautiful story.

Though I was not an expert in geology, I could see the story of this crack in the side of the mountain. Time, elements, and force had gotten the best of the rock, leaving an area of breakage along the side of the canyon. Rather than engineering a way to put the rock back together and hide the fault line, the crack was now part of the mountain, the joining of the traumatic past with the hopeful future. The canyon was a testament to the inevitability of change and the myth of durability.

I sat along the edge of the fault line for another hour or so, writing some thoughts in my journal. I reflected on some of the mistakes I made, events, words, and behaviors I was embarrassed to talk about, ashamed to admit. Some of my mistakes felt like aspects of teaching I should have remembered from college. I knew my lessons could have been better if I had taken the time to plan more thoroughly and anticipate when my students might need more time, more help, more direction. With more time or effort, I could have given the students assessments that aligned with what they were supposed to be learning rather than just keeping them busy. My classroom management strategies should have been focused on what students were doing right, catching them being good rather than punishing what they did wrong.

For the first time, I wasn't operating within the context of another teacher's system. I was creating my own rules, procedures, and culture, and I made a lot of mistakes along the way. My perception of teaching and the classroom had been molded by dozens of teachers over the span of nearly two decades, the apprenticeship of observation. Making my own teaching decisions for my own students revealed cracks in my armor, aspects of teaching I never had to think about until confronted with an unfamiliar situation. Remarkably I did not crumble into a pile of mortar in front of my horrified class. There were a couple of moments when I thought teaching would break me, but the patience, sagacity, and care of my colleagues was poured into those cracks like liquid gold. Mistakes became lessons, those lessons strengthened my character, and my character transformed into wisdom that can't be learned in a textbook or a lecture. My cracks became a point of pride, truth I could pass along to other new or future teachers. I endured one self-inflicted hardship after another yet finished the year proud of the progress I had made between August and May. After spending much of the fall semester in survival mode to the point of questioning my ability to teach, I knew the teacher sitting on this mountain in the cool, dry air was not the person who moved to Texas nine months prior.

I wrote some of these thoughts down in the journal, my own form of kintsugi. Each word was liquid gold, transforming each shameful experience into the wisdom that only comes from putting myself out there and being brave enough to struggle with something new. Not acknowledging the failures would dishonor a critical part of my story that deserved to be placed right alongside every success I ever had.

Glancing at my watch, I knew I had just enough time to hike back to the cabin, close everything up, and drive down the mountain in time for dinner. I whisked down the side of the canyon and back up to the cabin, where I locked the doors and windows and lowered the blinds. As I adjusted my seatbelt, I glanced out the window of my dad's truck for one last look at my favorite place on earth. I ascended the dirt road heading toward the highway, grateful for my cabin, for this canyon and its cracks, and for the golden opportunity to break and be repaired.

## CHAPTER 17 Boxes

AFTER FOUR YEARS AT TIMBERLINE, I got the itch for a new adventure. I had been accepted into two different graduate programs in Colorado, and I settled on CSU because I would have the opportunity to teach college courses. From the time I completed my application, received my acceptance letter, and made a campus visit in Fort Collins to meet the director of the graduate program, time creeped by like the second hand on a clock. Lessons, days, and weeks moved at half speed. I noticed everything around me as I wondered if this would be the last time I ever worked in a school. What if my graduate degree led to a career where I never worked with children again? I wish there was a word for the simultaneous feeling of excitement for a new opportunity and sadness for all you are leaving behind. Whatever you call that emotion, it was how I felt nearly all the time.

    I started packing up my classroom about two weeks before school was out. I had a short window of time between when school ended and my move to Colorado. I didn't have the heart to tell my class I was not returning to Timberline the next year, so I kept the packed boxes hidden in various closets and shelves in the fourth-grade pod. Once the kids were gone for the summer, I slowly brought all of the packed boxes back to my classroom and stacked them in the back of the classroom. Against the wall, about four boxes high and perhaps two or three deep, the stack was both imposing and impressive. How did I accumulate all of this stuff? I had games for the children to play, and hundreds of books I had gotten for free or at a deep discount from book order clubs, garage sales, and clearance tables at the bookstore. I didn't even want to think about how much of my own money I had spent on these supplies.

In a separate box, sitting on a table near the door, I had placed items dear to me after four years at this school. Notes from students and parents, recognitions, mementoes from field trips, and, of course, I had all of my sports pennants. The box was filled to the top, making it difficult to close. When I lifted it, I knew it would feel twice as heavy by the time I lugged it to my truck.

A monolith of boxes stacked on one side, a single box of treasures on the other. I was transported back to my first day in this classroom, to the sights, smells, sounds, and emotions of that day. I started with nothing. My possessions, my experiences, even my identity as a teacher were all raw materials, unrefined and lacking shape. I relived that trip to the teacher supply store, the scene of Carol and Freddy pulling up behind my broken-down truck on the highway, the picture of my teaching partners sitting at the table in the back of the room waiting to surprise me on my first birthday on my own. I owed so much of who I was, who I had become, to them. At different times, they had sheltered me, shielded me, and walked with me through the uncomfortable. A twinge of guilt caused me to shudder when I thought about how much effort I had required on their part. What could I possibly give them in return? How does a person repay a lifetime's worth of kindness and patience?

I knew the person taking my spot on the fourth-grade team was a first-year teacher. I had the opportunity to meet her during the interview process. She was excited and eager to get started, and I knew from her first words in the interview she would be fantastic as a teacher. I pictured her walking into this empty room for the first time, wondering, as I had, where to start. The room was silent except for the faint buzz of the new lights hanging from the ceiling. This room contained more memories than I could ever recall in a lifetime. I wondered what I would remember about this experience in ten years. I propped the door open with my foot, switched off the light, and picked up the one box I would take with me. The rest of the boxes were for the new teacher. I could at least make sure she had more to start with than I did.

The door clicked shut, and Carol and Linda were standing in the hallway waiting for me. Goodbyes are hard for me. I leaned back into my typical coping mechanism of assuring them I would come back to visit in a few months. They would never know I was gone. They both hugged me as they wiped tears from their eyes. There were no final words of wisdom, just reminders to stay safe on the road, to keep in touch, and to work hard in graduate school. I echoed my promise to stay in touch and come back to visit as soon as possible. I leaned down to pick up my stuff. I walked out of my very first classroom for the very last time holding nothing but a box.

# CHAPTER 18 Out of the Shadows

IN ONE OF HIS MORE WELL-KNOWN WORKS, Plato tells the allegory of prisoners chained and held captive in a cave. They are facing a blank wall of the cave, and behind them a fire is burning. As the prisoners' captors walk back and forth in front of the fire, they cast long shadows upon the blank wall. The prisoners, having never left the cave, believe the shadows are real and they begin naming the shapes they see. Over time, some of the prisoners manage to escape and discover life as it really is, while others, unable to envision a better life, stay in the cave, huddled in the dark, haunted and deluded by the shadows.

Was this the education I was providing my students? Most of us start off in a place we haven't chosen for ourselves, living sheltered, curated, protected lives. We do what we're told, stay within the purview of our care providers, and are shielded from the world. Whether it's bit by bit through a series of experiences or in an earth-shattering traumatic event, we come to understand that the world of shadows we saw through a glass darkly was only a representation of the way things really are. We learn not all people are looking out for us. We eventually comprehend the scale and commitment and sacrifice needed to truly invest ourselves in work that matters, in something that will outlive us. Lessons will not always be easily learned and may leave us apprehensive or fearful or discouraged.

We acknowledge the necessity of living and working in community with others, that life is a chorus not a monologue. For some, the world as it is may be too much to process, and they retreat back into the cave, sheltered from the wind and rain but also exiled from the healing warmth that comes from that first ray of light emerging from a frigid night. What is my role in helping my students step into the open air and embrace the love, loss, failure, victory, and unpredictability that comes with going all-in on things that matter?

Standing in front of my class, I watched them completing a worksheet I had somehow convinced them was an important investment of their time and energy. A shadow on the wall. I wondered if I was chained up alongside them, living someone else's life, naming the silhouettes, or was I standing at the mouth of the cave beckoning them to join me. Pulling back the bow, one lesson or experience at a time, I was ready to help them launch into the joy and pain of a life lived well. I wanted them to know, beyond their ability to learn math and spelling and geography, they had what it takes to endure the challenges that come from leaving the quiver and learning to fly.

# EPILOGUE *Dear Curby*

DEAR CURBY,

I HAVE THOUGHT BACK ON THIS MOMENT for more years than I care to admit. I remember the khaki pants, white shirt, blue and red striped tie, navy blazer, and brown penny loafers you are wearing right now. I know the black belt you're wearing doesn't match, but it's the only one you have at the moment. You were almost late today, and you're feeling less nervous than people expected you to feel. This is because you don't know what you don't know. Blissful ignorance. I remember the lunch you packed, and I know you won't eat very much of it. You are excited to start this new adventure, and you're lonely because you don't have anyone to share it with. I don't need to tell you, this will be your first experience of being completely on your own. I feel like I should tell you, you're not ready for it.

When I think about you, I rarely consider how far we've come. I tend to think about what I would tell you if I had the chance. So, here is my chance. I won't give you any advice because you wouldn't know where to put it. You barely know how to get from your apartment to the school, and if I gave you any pointers you would just stand there nodding and smiling, doing your best to be polite until I left so you could set them aside and get back to work on the stuff you think you should be doing. Whatever you do after you read this, trust me, it won't matter because this year was meant to be hard. The best thing you can do is open your eyes and your heart and try to remember as much as you can from this experience. I have put together a little toolbox that might help you make sense of this at some point down the road. Even as I look back on this reflection of myself, I can already see you changing before my eyes.

The first thing you need to know is that you will encounter opposition. Not all opposition is bad, even if it isn't pleasant. It will come in various forms, and you don't always have to fight against it. Sometimes the best response to opposition is to get out of its way and see where it's going. It may lead you to some place you had never considered.

The most common type of resistance will come in the form of people, which makes sense. As a teacher, you will spend nearly every daylight hour with other people, and there is no way you can please all of them at once.

You will work alongside all kinds of people experiencing all sorts of incidents. For starters, you will spend most of your time with nine- and ten-year-olds. They will think you're pretty cool most of the time, but they may not always listen to you, follow instructions, stay in their seats, stop talking, get along with each other, do their homework, or tell the truth. Children bring an element of delightful unpredictability into your life, but they may not always want to cooperate. Their parents are tired, stressed, over-caffeinated, under-exercised, worried, hopeful, anxious, entertained, and exasperated by their children, and chances are the child in your class is not the only one for whom they are trying to keep up with their physical, mental, social, and emotional development. Your colleagues who are parents are likely experiencing all of these things, as well, and they are doing it while spending the entire day with someone else's children. To top it all off, your principal is trying to manage all of these people at once, while also trying to live their own life. A school is this diverse milieu of beautifully imperfect people all working together to do what's best for children, so things might get messy at times.

There is no way I can try to encompass every possible interpersonal dynamic you will experience this year, but there are two lessons you can learn from every person you meet. First, no matter how they treat you or respond to you, it's most likely not about you. Whether they are generous and kind or aggressive and rude, it is not because of anything you did. If you find your interactions with someone to be enjoyable, be thankful for it and don't take it for granted. If your interaction is less than pleasant, learn from it and try not to take it personally. Just like a wounded animal will snap at the hand trying to help it, some people will push you away or try to give you a reason for leaving them alone. You will have to use your judgment about how to respond, but no matter what, don't take it personally. Whether another person's words and actions make you want to puff out your chest or hide under a table, just keep it in perspective.

The other opportunity you have to learn from your interactions with others is humility. The way other people treat you does not determine your value, for better or worse. Even if your worth is not entangled in someone else's opinion of you, there may be something to learn from them. They may have a perspective you have never before considered, or they may reveal, whether intentionally or not, something about yourself you never knew. It could be in the words you use, or the jokes you tell, or the expression on your face when they are telling you about their day. You may have to sift through some interpersonal debris to get to the nugget of truth, but other people can help you see yourself from an unexplored angle if you will stay humble and open-minded.

Another form of opposition you will encounter is logistics. At times you will come up with a plan so clever, you will swear it rode into your imagination on a bolt of lightning sent from Thor himself. This idea will consume you, occupy your dreams, and annoy everyone who you happen to see for the next eight days, but unless you start to put it into action, it will slowly fade away. No matter how much you want to make this idea come to life, you will find yourself short on time, energy, money, support, and the help of other people to make it happen. The stars will rarely, if ever, perfectly align for an idea to become real. The only way to make it real is through hard work and innovative thinking. There are no shortcuts or mind tricks. Difficult logistics does not mean an idea was not meant to be. It's a way for you to assess how much you are willing to work to turn that idea into reality.

People and logistics may seem to be the only barriers you will encounter, but your greatest source of opposition will be yourself. You will have doubts and other times be overconfident. You will fail to plan and other times stick too rigidly to the plans you made. You will sometimes over analyze what other people are thinking and talk yourself out of making a move, and other times you will make too many assumptions, leap too soon, and wish you had spent more time thinking it through. Sometimes your fear will cause you not to trust people, and other times you will place too much trust in other people's opinions about you. Have faith in others and have faith in yourself.

Another helpful hint I would like to pass along is that you will experience failure. You will encounter more new experiences this year than at any time in your life. A new job, a new city, and a new beginning. Sometimes the only way to learn is to do it wrong the first time. You will take many wrong turns, explain concepts incorrectly, start in the wrong place, and aim for the wrong target. There is no shame in doing a new thing wrong the first time. There are many mistakes you need to make.

Of course, you are expecting to experience this kind of failure. The type you will have a much harder time dealing with is when you fail to do what you know you should have done and didn't for one reason or another. While failing forward has the potential, with the right mindset, to produce hope, the failure of missed opportunities leads to regret. You will experience plenty of these failures, as well. Phone calls returned too late or never at all, notes with no response, relationships where you never followed up or asked enough questions or revealed how you really felt. This kind of failure produces hurt feelings, disillusionment, confusion and mixed messages, and a lack of trust.

There is no question that vulnerability can be risky. You never know how someone will respond to the power and passion of unprocessed emotions, but the reward of connection and affirmation is worth putting yourself out there. You have a tendency to create a façade of perfection and self-protection, and all that does is leave you isolated and lonely. When you're locked in your perfection chamber, the only thing you hear is your own thoughts, and I hate to break it to you, most of them are unhelpful and untrue. The work you are doing as a teacher will require your whole heart, and the best place to start is by not protecting yourself. Tell your students you're proud of them, praise them every single time they do something right, and let them call their parents with good news. Tell your colleagues how much you appreciate their help and support. Tell your friends you love them and value having them in your life. Your vibrant vulnerability may take some getting used to, but the people you care about will soon see it as part of your personality, just another dimension of who you are.

The last piece of advice I would like to impart while I still have your attention is that you consider recalibrating how you define success. Your life up to this point has been spent in a fabricated success factory. I'm not saying you didn't work hard to earn the accomplishments you've had up to this point, and they have helped you get to where you are right now. Consider your accomplishments up to now as guideposts along a clear, well-marked trail. As long as you stayed on the path and kept up your pace, you were bound to reach the guideposts. Assignments led to grades, which led to a GPA and the honor roll, which helped determine your class ranking. All of these guideposts facilitated your entrance to college, then all you had to do was swap these guideposts for other guideposts.

Now that you're off this clearly marked trail, you will have to create your own guideposts. There are no more grades or honor rolls. There are occasional awards and recognitions, but as a new teacher you aren't even eligible for them yet. Teacher of the year, of the month, of the week, of the half day. You're not there yet.

You will have moments when you feel success or when you are recognized, such as being asked to speak at a meeting or recording a song for other new teachers. Don't take these seldom moments for granted, but these markers should not be how you judge whether or not you're doing a good job.

For your first year, a better measure of your success as a teacher is whether you're able to keep up with the pace. Teaching has its own rhythm, and if all you have to do is plan lessons, teach, and grade papers, then you would be able to keep up. It just so happens there is a lot more to this job than that. Every six weeks you will have to evaluate every student in every subject. We'll call that the report card, and there is a lot more to this process than what you remember as a student. On top of that, you will need to come up with awards and recognitions for all of your students every six weeks, then present those awards at an assembly in front of all your students' parents. Just when you recover from the early mornings and late nights required to prepare the report cards and awards assembly, you will turn around and start getting ready for the next six-week grading period.

Academic recognitions are not the only time when you will have to put forth extra time and effort. You will need to think about field trips, enrichment activities, figure out what to do with your corner of the school garden, and don't forget about the fourth-grade program you have to perform at a PTA meeting each year. Oh, and you will be the one in charge of planning all the music, since you know how to play the guitar. There will be holiday parties, guest speakers, standardized testing, and school-wide initiatives like Red Ribbon Week. Just when you think you can stop to catch your breath, there is another event coming up.

Let me tell you, these events are not for you, and they are all worth it. These special memories are what your students remember when they think about their time in school. They'll also remember you and a lot of the content you taught them, but when they reminisce about fourth grade, these events will make them smile. They will eventually tell their children about their field trips and other memorable days, so don't cut any corners. Do your best to run the race well so you look back on the year proud of the experiences you created for your students. In other words, you are now a conduit between your students and what is possible. Lean in, embrace it, and enjoy the fireworks.

Be careful because you can only keep up this pace in short bursts. You will have weeks that seem to drag on forever. You will eventually learn to plan ahead and use the slow weeks to get a head start on the busy weeks. You will have some weeks where you wonder how you will get everything done, and you will kick yourself for not making more progress when you still had time. There will be some early mornings, a lot of long days, and quite a few late nights. You will come home on Fridays thankful for the weekend ahead, and you will go to bed on Sundays wondering where it all went. Just when you think you are about to crash and burn, along comes Thanksgiving, then Christmas and New Years, then Spring Break. The pace is frenetic at times, exhausting, and since you have never been in this experience before, the horizon will always seem obscure. Just trust me, it's out there and a break will always come just when you need it most.

Here's the secret: wake up every morning, put one foot in front of the other until you are in your classroom, then keep going until it's time to head back home for the night. You will be tired, you will get frustrated and disillusioned, you will be embarrassed by your own incompetence—your inability at times to anticipate the obvious—and you may even start to fantasize about your next dream career. All of this is natural, and even though it doesn't seem like it, your willingness to trudge through the drudgery of the work week even when you feel like a failure is growing you in ways you can't measure. You will learn humility, patience, and stamina. You will learn to hang in there just a little longer until things get better. Life will sometimes lead to the mountaintops, the pinnacle of success. You will often race through the valleys, tending to one field then another then another. In between those moments, you will learn to lumber through the mundane without letting it sap you of your joy and hope. All three of these contexts are part of the landscape of being a teacher.

So, that's it. Simple advice that we get to spend the rest of our life internalizing, practicing, and learning. Always strive to do what is best for your students and be a guardian of their potential. Everything else is just window dressing, and I can't think of anything else to include in this letter. Well, just one last thing. In the fall of 1998, you will be at church mingling with some friends on a calm Sunday morning. In the minutes before you teach your young adult Bible study, a friend of yours, Sheri, will introduce you to her roommate. After a few minutes of chatting, you say, "It was nice to meet you," and you go your separate ways. Just let her go, and proceed with whatever plans you have been making. I only ask you to remember her face. That is all you will need to remember.

BEST OF LUCK,
CURBY

# ACKNOWLEDGEMENTS

IT HARDLY SEEMS FAIR that only one name goes on the cover of a project like this. Every story, every word of this book has been touched by someone else, and the person who wrote them would not be who he is without the influence of so many wonderful people over the years. I have so many people to thank, and if I happen to leave someone out, offer me grace and know that, in the words of Taylor Swift, "this is me trying."

First, I would like to thank the teachers and students I have worked with throughout my career as an educator. I talk a lot about my relationship with Carol Cate and Linda Perkins in this book, but there were other teachers and leaders who have been equally supportive and influential in my development as a teacher. In no particular order, I would like to thank Bennie Gilliam, Lisa Dunn, Jamie Youngbauer, Jana Thomson, Sandee Williams, Leslie Madden, and Patty Arner. We started as strangers, we transformed into colleagues, and I now consider you lifelong friends (whether we keep in touch or not).

Regarding my students, you will be harder to name. There are just so many of you, and I have limited space to write. To every student who passed through my room at Timberline, Willard, CSU, Casper College, PVCC, UVA, UIS, UNT, and TCU, you all played a part in shaping me into a better teacher. I'm grateful for the opportunity to work with you and learn just a little more about teaching and learning, about being human, and about myself.

I have also worked with many talented and brilliant colleagues at each of the universities with which I am affiliated. Again, there are too many of you to name, but I value your support and inspiration as I have worked to become the best professor and colleague I know how to be. Just when I think I have nothing more to achieve, you show me that more is possible.

I would also like to thank my parents and grandparents for their support during my first teaching position. For my parents, Ron and Gale, you showed me what it looks like to stick with my goals and to take risks, and you are still my biggest cheering section. I definitely won the parent lottery, and I love you more than you know. To my grandparents, John, Ella Jean, Lloyd, and Mary, I miss you and wish you were here to see this. I can hear Big Mama bragging to her friends in heaven as I write this.

The unsung heroes of my early years as a teacher are my friends, the OG E-town crew: Brent, David, Brandie, Charmaine, Amy, and Brian. You adopted me into your ad hoc family, and I haven't shut up since. Now you know what happens when you coax a shy introvert out of his shell.

The first person to read the first draft of this book, besides my mother, was Pam Elise Harris. Your positive feedback and encouragement are the reason I decided to keep pursuing this project until I found a publisher.

To the TCU Press team—Dan, Kathy, Abigail, James, and Marco—thank you for the opportunity to put these stories out for the world to read. Your feedback, revisions, and commitment to my book have been invaluable.

Finally, I want to thank my family. The majority of these words were written while you were still sleeping in the other end of the house. I don't deserve a family as loving and gracious as you, and you don't deserve a person who snores and tells such terrible jokes. Thank you for keeping me around. To my sons, Sam and Nate, thank you for keeping me young and active. You are everything I prayed for when I found out I was having sons, and you have turned out to be more than I knew to ask for. I'll never forget when you told me, "I think if we went to school together, we would have been friends." I think you're right.

Finally, to my wife, Gina—I don't even want to consider my life had I not remembered your face.

# ABOUT THE AUTHOR

CURBY ALEXANDER is an Associate Professor of Professional Practice in the TCU College of Education. He began his career as a teacher in Grapevine, TX, and throughout his time as a public educator he taught several different grades and had many roles. Curby has spent the last eighteen years teaching at the university level, where he now helps prepare aspiring teachers for a career as professional educators. Curby is a proud alum of Utah State University, Colorado State University, and the University of Virginia. When he isn't teaching, Curby spends as much time as possible with his wife Gina and their twin sons, Sam and Nate. *Chalk Dust* is his first book.

www.ingramcontent.com/pod-product-compliance
Lightning Source LLC
Chambersburg PA
CBHW031501160426
43195CB00010BB/1061